fix
this
ne**x**t

FOR
REAL ESTATE
INVESTORS

B. SCOTT TODD
FOREWORD BY MIKE MICHALOWICZ

ISBN (paperback): 979-8-9999519-0-8
ISBN (ebook): 979-8-9999519-1-5

Disclaimer:
The information contained within this book is for informational
purposes only. It should not be considered financial, legal, or tax
advice. You should seek the services of an attorney or tax professional
to determine what may be best for your individual needs.

Page design and typesetting: CB Messer (www.cbmesser.com)
Copy editor: Zoë Bird

This book is dedicated to those who are brave enough to chase their dreams and foolish enough to never stop.

CONTENTS

Foreword

vii

Introduction

1

Chapter 1

THE ROAD TO FREEDOM

7

Chapter 2

FIND IT AND FIX IT

29

Chapter 3

ESTABLISH PREDICTABLE DEAL FLOW

53

Chapter 4

CREATE PERMANENT PROFIT

81

Chapter 5

ACHIEVE ORGANIZATIONAL ORDER

107

Chapter 6

FROM GETTING TO GIVING

135

Chapter 7

FROM TRANSACTION TO TRANSFORMATION

143

Chapter 8

LEAVE YOUR LEGACY

171

Chapter 9

YOU'RE GONNA DO SOMETHING BIG

195

Endnotes

203

Acknowledgments

209

About the Author

213

FOREWORD

THE GRASS ALWAYS SEEMS GREENER ON THE OTHER SIDE OF THE fence. If you are new to real estate investing, it might look like the lushest, easiest, most lucrative path to earning passive income: Sit back, relax, and watch the money pour in.

But if you are already on the other side of the fence, you know the real story. Although real estate investing can absolutely provide financial freedom, it also demands hard work, resilience, and the ability to navigate constant market shifts and unexpected challenges. Too often, investors find themselves trapped in a cycle of reacting to urgent issues without a clear plan. I call this the "survival trap," a never-ending loop of putting out fires, doing constant damage control, and hoping it all comes together. Without a framework to follow, that cycle drains your time, money, and energy.

Yes, real estate investing can be the best financial move you ever make, but only if you know what to do and when to do it.

Enter Scott Todd. If you are not already familiar with him, Scott is known for his deep expertise, resilience, and ability to simplify complex real estate strategies into actionable steps. Scott and I first met when he hosted me on a podcast to discuss my book *Clockwork*. What started as a conversation about business efficiency quickly turned into something more. That day, I gained a deep respect for his insight, his methodical approach to problem-solving, and his commitment to helping entrepreneurs succeed.

Scott's story is one I suspect will have touches of familiarity for you. He was the kid who dreamed of owning his own business, the neighborhood entrepreneur who always looked for new opportunities. But like many, he followed the traditional path. He earned an accounting degree, an MBA, and a postgraduate certificate from MIT Sloan. He climbed the corporate ladder, gaining experience in sales, finance, operations, and IT and eventually becoming the vice president of IT at a Fortune 300 company. By any external measure, he had made it.

Yet the entrepreneurial itch never left him. That is the part I relate to. Choosing MIT... not so much.

In 2016, when his department was outsourced, Scott was ready. He had already started building a real estate investing business that would replace his corporate income. But when he went all in, he faced the same challenges that many new investors encounter. He felt overwhelmed by the endless tasks, struggled to prioritize, and realized that entrepreneurship was much more demanding than he had expected (I relate to that part too). But Scott did not just overcome these challenges. He transformed them into opportunities for growth and learning.

Today, Scott leads one of the largest firms in his investing niche and dedicates his time to helping other real estate investors achieve the financial freedom they desire. His diverse experience across multiple domains aligns perfectly with the principles I teach in *Fix This Next*. He understands that, like any other startup, a new real estate venture faces competing challenges. The lack of a clear framework for addressing them leads straight into the survival trap—a guaranteed way to build a business that does not work.

Fix This Next for Real Estate Investors builds upon the Business Priority Pyramid I created. Here, Scott introduces the Investor's Priority Pyramid, a tool designed to help investors identify and focus on their business's most pressing needs. This approach guides you out of the day-to-day grind of putting out fires, helping you pinpoint the most important thing to fix next instead. It ensures that your efforts lead to sustainable growth and, ultimately, the time freedom you have been working toward.

Scott's insights and strategies are the real deal. They are born from real-world experience and have been tested in the trenches of real estate investing. By the end of this book, you will have a clear framework for identifying your business's most pressing needs. And as a result, you will be able to achieve the dream of every real estate investor, new or experienced: predictable, passive income and true time freedom.

As you read these pages, be ready to shift your perspective, embrace a structured approach to problem-solving, and take actionable steps toward building a business that serves you. You are about to live a life by design. Your new and improved real estate investing journey starts now.

—MIKE MICHALOWICZ

INTRODUCTION

The email subject line caught my attention. My assistant normally handles my inbox, but this one seemed important. Out of curiosity, I opened it to find Jonathan's message: "Please cancel all subscriptions for my email address. My business is closing…"

I routinely hear sad stories like this—yet another investor leaving the business. I tried once to determine the failure rate of real estate investors, and the best source I could find was a post on a real estate forum that claimed it is 90-95%. I think that number is a little high, but unfortunately, it might be close.

Still, Jonathan shutting down his business caught me by surprise for some reason, and I wanted to know why. I met him after speaking at an event when he walked up to me, introduced himself, and we talked for a while. He's a great guy. His real estate investment goal was to replace his income so he could spend more time with his wife and four kids.

I replied to Jonathan, "I'm sorry to hear you are closing your business. Can I ask why?" I hoped that he would respond but doubted he would. Over the years, I have asked other investors the same question many times, and I rarely get a response. It is like they have closed the book on that part of their life and are on to the next chapter. I can relate to that mindset because I was a statistic, too; my first four forays into real estate investing did not work out. I understand and respect when other investors take a hit and move on. We each handle the roller coaster differently.

Later in the day, I checked my inbox and saw that Jonathan actually had replied. His write-up was detailed, an excellent post-mortem review, but here's the important part: "I tried to do everything myself instead of hiring some help. I also focused on forming an LLC, worrying about a website, and paying for too many systems that I was not using. I tried to solve problems before they became problems. Soon, I became frustrated and quit marketing and mailing. I got burnt out going at it alone…"

I've seen Jonathan's story repeated so many times. It's painful. And every time, as I remember my own investing failures, I can feel these investors' hopes and dreams fading into the sunset. I have more exposure to these stories than most because I have taught nearly 2,000 entrepreneurs how to use real estate as their way to freedom. I've seen them on their first days in the business and sometimes witness their last. Each time one of them moves on, I hear their dreams shouting, *Please don't give up on me!*

As a real estate investor entrepreneur, you share the same pains and struggles as any other founder. One of the most common is being overwhelmed. You start with a thought, a dream, a goal. It lives in your head, and then you give it life. You take something intangible and manifest it in the physical world by doing something that most people never will: starting a company. According to research by Statista, you are in a small group. Only 7% of adults in the United States own and operate a business.[1]

Starting a company is hard. You have a lot to do to get it off the ground. As Jonathan wrote, there are LLCs to form, a website to create, mailing and marketing to do, and systems to build. And that's just the big stuff—there are hundreds, if not thousands, of micro-tasks that also need your attention. Not to mention juggling all this with your day job and your personal life.

Between the tasks, the job, and family obligations, you begin to feel tired and burnt out. Self-doubt creeps in and you start questioning everything. Your inner critic-trolls know you are on the ropes, so they line up to take turns taunting you. You try to do and fix everything, yet the list keeps getting longer and it feels like there is no light at the end of the tunnel. Maintaining the fight takes grit, perseverance, and a burning desire; if the trolls catch you in an exhausted, beaten-down moment, it's easy to tap out and quit.

Seeing the very opportunity that gave you hope and excitement about achieving your dreams begin to suck the life from you is crushing. I've been on that roller coaster and it's not fun, but there is hope and a path forward.

I first got the real estate bug in 1994 and made five attempts at becoming a professional investor. The first four tries never quite took off, forcing me to stay in my day job. In late 2014, I decided to give real estate investing one more try. Unlike the previous four attempts, I needed this venture to work. My time in corporate America was running out. I had to take my shot.

Nine months later, I still struggled to gain traction, my inner critic-trolls were beating me down, and I was close to quitting.

In that moment of weakness, though, I discovered a system that worked for me and realized that I had the skills and confidence to navigate these challenges. My system, pulled together from years of experience managing global teams, was based on prioritizing the most important activities in the business. This homegrown approach finally gave me the traction I needed to break out. I overcame the resistance and eventually, after developing and refining that system, achieved my dreams of time and income freedom.

That final, successful attempt at real estate investing began with $10,000. Seventeen months later, it became my full-time gig. It was a twenty-year journey from my first exposure to real estate investing to the life of my dreams. I want that life for you now, not in twenty years.

My first exposure to Mike Michalowicz was through his book *Profit First*. In 2020, when Mike released *Fix This Next*, I ordered it immediately and it quickly became one of my favorite books. Then I went back and read *The Pumpkin Plan* and reread *Clockwork*. All of them are great books, but I felt an instant, deep connection with *Fix This Next*. What captivated me was that Mike had managed to codify the steps I had taken to gain traction in the early days of my business. It was as if he had watched what I did and found a way to both eloquently translate and polish the process.

Mike's *Fix This Next* process was great, but I felt it lacked the pieces I needed as a real estate investor. Like a chef using another recipe as a base, I began to build my own version of Fix This Next. I tweaked Mike's process and framework, adding the core needs that apply to us and removing the ones that don't. I modified the system to address the greatest challenge facing all real estate entrepreneurs: completing all of those tasks. I made it work for us.

So, after reading Jonathan's reply, I called him and we spoke. I asked him to reconsider. "Don't do it. Don't throw in the towel. I have an idea!"

But I was too late. As I suspected, he was on to his next chapter.

Jonathan summarized the struggle: "I have never been an entrepreneur and had no idea that I and I alone would determine how my business would succeed or fail. I guess I didn't realize how much time and effort this would take."

I wrote this book to share my approach with the real estate investing community. I need to share it with you and do my part to reduce the number of investors who quit and move on to another chapter. If you struggle to get it all done, there is a solution. Rather than run from emergency to emergency and try to handle everything, identify which problem you need to fix next. You will learn how to do just that in this book.

Does my system work? I began applying my version of Fix This Next, which I call "Fix This Next for Real Estate Investors (FTNREI)," to my investing business in 2020. When I did, my business took off. From 2020 to 2024, we increased our revenue 1,000%, becoming one of the largest investment firms in our space.

Achieving growth of this nature produces a lot of growing pains. Every day, we were hit with new challenges and new fires to put out. Knowing we couldn't solve all the issues at once, and applying the FTNREI principles, we addressed our most pressing problems first.

Through teaching, I have seen those who follow the FTNREI approach also gain traction more quickly. It has worked for me and many others, and it will work for you. By the end of this book, you will have a framework to identify your business's most pressing needs so you can replace your income and achieve time freedom.

Chapter I

THE ROAD
TO FREEDOM

WILL I EVER BE ABLE TO REPLACE MY INCOME AND GET OUT OF HERE?

I wondered that almost daily, but on this July day, my desire to break free from the grips of corporate America was particularly strong. It also seemed impossible. Only nine months into my real estate investment side hustle, I was ready to shut it down. Between the demands of a challenging corporate job and a busy family life, finding time to grow my side hustle was difficult. The list of tasks on my to-do list was growing, and it was hard to keep up. Easy tasks were quickly resolved, but many seemed insurmountable.

I felt like a circus juggler, mailing letters, pricing properties, completing due diligence, marketing properties, making sales, managing client payments, doing the accounting—and I was getting overwhelmed. My friends in the business told me, "Hire a virtual assistant," and I did. But naturally I needed to train them, and training meant yet another task on my list. Then my friends said, "Record your work. Make systems."

Great, I'll add those to the list. As the business grew, it required more and more of my time. Real estate investing was supposed to give me more time and more money, and neither were anywhere in sight. The time commitment needed to grow the business was taking time and money away from my family, which was in direct conflict with why I started it in the first place.

In addition to feeling like I was drowning in my investment business, I felt like my corporate job, the one that fed my family, was at risk. I had seen the writing on the wall ten months before, when the CEO of the company resigned for "personal reasons." The new CEO brought along a stream of new executives. Their first goal was simple: Replace the old leaders.

What followed was a predictable sequence of events; each new executive brought their friends and then put them into key roles. My new boss was on the friend list. He came in as a vice president and my title was also vice president. It doesn't take a rocket scientist to know that a vice president doesn't report to another vice president for long. Despite nine years of stellar performance and increasing responsibilities, I knew as soon as the old CEO left and the new team arrived that my time at the company was limited.

When the news broke that the old CEO was gone, I realized: *This is my shot.* I had always wanted to work for myself and had attempted to start many businesses in my life, but none of them ever took flight. But somehow, I knew this time would be different; I was going to turn a real estate investing side hustle into my exit vehicle. This business would be the one that allowed me to replace my income and achieve the freedoms I desired. At least, I hoped it would.

But on this day, my boss of two months amped up the pressure. During his staff meeting, he blamed me for not preventing a major system outage—which was caused by another team managed by his friend. The truth was, it was my team that quickly diagnosed and resolved the issue. We weren't the cause; we were the solution.

I wanted so badly to have my investment business up and running so I could finally make the leap from my corporate job, but it was still so new, there was a lot of work to be done, and I wasn't anywhere close to replacing my income. Time was running out. The fastest way out of this job would be to get another job, and a new job would require more of my time getting up to speed. That meant I would need to close or suspend the investment business. But getting a new job would also mean giving up on my dreams of financial and time freedom once again.

At the end of the workday, I decided to go for a walk before dinner and cool my jets before making a potentially irrational decision. I was in Oklahoma City traveling for work, so I drove to a large park on Lake Hefner, which is a large reservoir. The park has a long walking trail around the lake, about a ten-mile loop. I had been to this park many times and never walked the entire trail, but today I considered it.

Besides the brutal workday, the weather made a long walk even harder. At 6:00 p.m., it was still ridiculously hot, more than 100º F, and the winds were more than twenty miles per hour. It felt as if I was being blasted by a giant blow dryer. It was miserable. The heat and the wind combined made it next to impossible to breathe. But I didn't want to leave; I needed to think.

WE DREAM OF FINANCIAL AND TIME FREEDOM

As I walked, all I could think about was replacing my income and how far off that seemed. Each day created exponentially more work for me in the business. Each new property I acquired required more time for due diligence, marketing, and sales tasks. These were just tasks to keep my head above water, let alone perform the work needed to build the company.

But then an important thought came to me: *You've only been at this for nine months. You can't expect to replace your income in such a short time frame.* I was getting some traction in my business, and it was slowly growing; I just wanted it to move faster. I felt I should be further along, the work was stacking up with no end in sight, and my inner-critic trolls questioned how it would all get done before I was downsized.

Today, in the workshops and classes I teach, I hear the same from my students. They will say, for example, "My customers ask me about my website. I don't have one, so I'm working on that now."

My reply is, "Oh, is that the most important thing you need to do to move you closer to your goal?"

Or I'll hear, "I need to create a logo, rehab the property, sell it, create systems, hire people, and close more deals. How do I do it all?"

My reply is the same: "What is the most pressing issue?"

Investors are drawn to real estate investing because they desire financial freedom and the associated time freedom it affords. That is why we are here.

But then reality hits: You are starting a business. Achieving those freedoms will require you and your team to complete a lot of tasks, solve a lot of problems, and build a lot of systems. It's easy to get overwhelmed by all the aspects of starting, running, and growing the business. As a result, it's not uncommon for investors like us to struggle to identify which issue to tackle next.

TACTICS AND TECHNIQUES

To OVERCOME THESE START-UP CHALLENGES and figure out what to do next, it's common to turn to a coach, consult other investors, and even seek advice from people with questionable experience through online forums.

Coaches are a great resource if they have experience solving the issues you are facing. I believe you can classify coaches into three categories: gurus, dorus, and newrus. Gurus are the ones who have done it in the past but shifted to providing coaching services and selling information. Dorus are the coaches who continue to operate their businesses while also providing supportive coaching services. Newrus are the new investors who are still learning but think they are qualified to coach you anyway.

All the resources you might consult are good at sharing tactics and techniques that work now or worked in the past. But tactics and techniques will only get you so far. What you need is a framework that will help you prioritize what issue to work on next. Once you know what problem to address, you can apply the correct tactic to solve it. But when you address the wrong one at the wrong time, you enter a survival trap—and to avoid that, you need a compass.

WE ALL NEED A COMPASS

PILOTS LOOK UP AT THE sky hoping for one thing: clear skies. They also know that it is not always possible to fly in ideal weather. They refer to less than favorable conditions such as fog, low clouds, or low visibility as "instrument meteorological conditions," or IMC. Flying in IMC requires hours of specialized training and an instrument rating, which is earned after passing a number of tests. It is every pilot's responsibility to know the weather throughout their flight path. If the weather will be IMC and they are not instrument rated, they are not permitted to fly.

On July 16, 1999, John F. Kennedy Jr. (JFK Jr.), the son of former US President John F. Kennedy; his wife, Carolyn Bessette-Kennedy; and her sister, Lauren Bessette, departed Essex County Airport, a small airfield less than an hour from New York City, in a Piper Saratoga piloted by JFK Jr.

They had intended to depart around 6:00 p.m., fly up the coast, and then cross over to Martha's Vineyard, an island located seven miles off the coast of Cape Cod, Massachusetts. Upon arriving at Martha's Vineyard, Lauren would deplane and JFK Jr. and Carolyn would continue on to Hyannis Port, Massachusetts.

The plan quickly unraveled, as the sisters arrived at the airport two hours and thirty minutes later than expected. The original plan would have allowed the group to depart during daylight hours; however, because of the late passengers, they departed at 8:38 p.m., well after sunset. This meant that the flight occurred at night.

JFK Jr. followed the coastline north and then began turning toward water, heading to Martha's Vineyard. As they flew over the water, the conditions below became hazy, obscuring some of the lights on the ground. Instead of turning back toward the coast and canceling the flight, they pressed on. According to a commercial airline pilot flying a Boeing 737 into nearby Boston that night, it was "very dark, no stars, no lights."[2] Flying over water in very dark conditions requires pilots to use their instrument flying skills. Unfortunately, JFK Jr. had very little experience flying at night. Nor was he instrument rated, which means he did not have full training on how to conduct a flight by the instruments alone.

One of the vital lessons that instrument-rated pilots learn is to always trust their instruments over their intuition. When pilots enter clouds or other situations that cause them to lose horizonal or ground references, they can experience spatial disorientation. Spatial disorientation occurs when a pilot receives conflicting signals from their inner ear and the surrounding visual cues.

When a pilot suffers from spatial disorientation, they can have false perceptions of the plane's orientation. They might think the plane is turning when it's flying straight and level. These false perceptions can cause the pilot to adjust the aircraft when no adjustments are needed. If the pilot fails to rely on their instruments and instead adjusts based on their senses, they can enter a graveyard spin. As you can imagine, a graveyard spin causes a plane to turn downward in circles until it hits the ground.

As JFK Jr. approached Martha's Vineyard, he began his initial descent and then turned right, toward the south. That put the coastline of Martha's Vineyard—and any trace of a horizon—behind him. Flying over a dark ocean requires skill and trust in your instruments. As the plane continued to descend, haze reduced the visibility in the area to less than two miles, meaning that JFK Jr. needed to rely on his instruments. He performed a series of turns to the left, then to the right, and the plane sped up, descending at first about 900 feet per minute and finally approaching 4,700 feet per minute as it spiraled down into the ocean. JFK Jr. had suffered from spatial disorientation and guided the plane into the dreaded graveyard spin.

According to the US Federal Aviation Administration, "Between 5 to 10 percent of all general aviation accidents can be attributed to spatial disorientation, 90 percent of which are fatal."[3]

The best tool a pilot has when entering IMC is trust in their instruments. The simplest instrument they use to ensure that they do not turn in the wrong direction is a compass. Just like pilots, you and your business need a compass. Research has shown that without reference points, humans are wired to go in circles;[4] we need something to keep us moving in the desired direction. Your business, too, needs a way to stop you from moving in circles.

When we are faced with multiple pressing issues to work on, how do we identify the most important one? Without a compass or tool, we tend to act as untrained pilots do when they fly into IMC. We follow our gut without first identifying what the business needs most.

Most of the time, simply reacting fails to move your business in the direction that is best for its long-term health. Solving the wrong problem at the wrong time can push your business in the wrong direction and cause you to enter a survival trap.

THE SURVIVAL TRAP

IN HIS BOOK *FIX THIS NEXT*,[5] Mike Michalowicz introduced the concept of the survival trap. This situation occurs when you are caught in a loop of constantly putting out the fire in front of you without first considering the larger business need.

To illustrate, take Sarah, a new investor. She recently purchased her first investment property, a single-family house she plans to hold as a rental.

After closing, Sarah determines that the house will need more repairs than she anticipated. These unplanned repairs will eat into her budget. Let's consider this point A in the figure below; think *A* for actual situation.

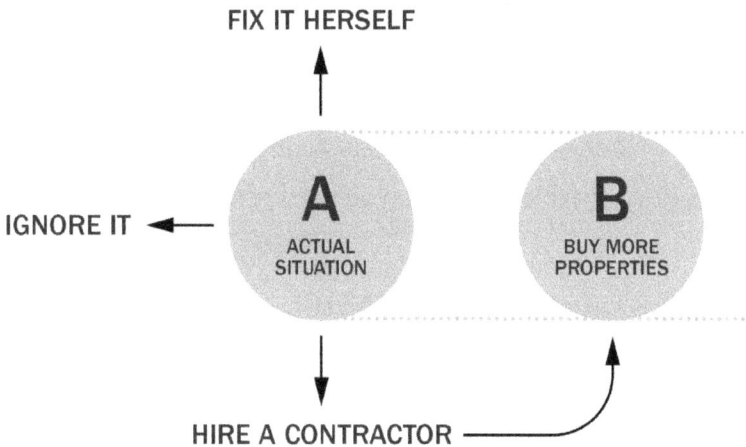

FIX IT HERSELF

IGNORE IT

A
ACTUAL
SITUATION

B
BUY MORE
PROPERTIES

HIRE A CONTRACTOR

Figure 1: Survival Trap

Sarah has a few choices: hire a contractor, make the repair herself, or ignore it. Sarah decides to put on her work clothes and make the repair herself. She figures that this will save her some money on the repair.

Sarah's long-term vision for her business is to increase her cash flow by building a portfolio of units. Her vision is point B in the figure; think *B* for business need.

When Sarah donned her work clothes and entered the world of maintenance and repairs, she also unknowingly entered a survival trap. The decision allowed her to save money, but it failed to allow her time to focus on the long-term need of the business, which was researching her next property. Saying yes to handyman duties forced her to say no to growing her portfolio.

Without a compass that can point you to your next most important task, you are destined to get bogged down by work that actually keeps you from that most important next task. Like the untrained pilot who enters IMC and fails to rely on their compass, you enter looping circles that move you further away from what your business truly needs. Rather than trying to put out fires and handle everything at once, identify which problem you need to fix next.

THE PRAGMATIC ENTREPRENEUR

AFTER WALKING TWO MILES IN the dry heat in Oklahoma City, I was ready to turn back. But instead of wanting to give up on my business, I felt like charging forward. As I headed back to the car, the words of one of my early bosses came to mind—during a performance review, he told me I was very pragmatic. I was impressed; I didn't even know what that meant. He said, "Your ability to prioritize the important stuff is fantastic. You quickly identify the important tasks and always seem to choose the right problem to solve."

Wait a minute, I thought, *If I break down all the tasks that need to be completed and prioritize them in the right sequence, I can create a snowball effect.* I realized that the snowball would allow me to move faster and faster; I just needed to identify and prioritize the most important things.

And there it was: I had been in a trap—a survival trap. I had been chasing down every problem without considering the larger business needs.

When problems are in front of us, we have a desire to solve them now. But not every problem is important today, and some are never important enough to solve. Every business has problems, and our job is to address the ones whose resolution will have the greatest impact first.

Additionally, I told myself that pursuing another job was a trap. Sure, it would get me out of this one, but I'd probably hate it just as much. If I kept working on my business, though, and prioritizing the greatest need, I could keep my dreams alive; you don't lose unless you quit.

Then I saw the bigger issue: Chasing after the solution to today's problem doesn't serve the business—it pushes you into the survival trap. To get out of that trap, you need a system.

THE FTN SYSTEM

In *Fix This Next*,[6] Mike Michalowicz introduced a system with the same name. The foundation of this system builds on the work of American psychologist Abraham Maslow, whose hierarchy of needs theory suggests that humans have five levels of needs.

1. *Physiological needs*—This is our base level of needs, the basic things we need to live, like food, water, shelter, sleep. Without these things, we cannot attend to our other needs.
2. *Safety needs*—With our basic needs meet, we can focus on our personal safety and security. Our financial security is also addressed in this level.
3. *Social needs*—Our social needs are important, but clearly not as important as food and water. After our basic needs are meet

and we feel safe, we start to find other people to be with and communities to join. We can't achieve this level until our other needs are met.

4. *Self-esteem needs*—After we find our people, we can work on gaining the recognition, status, and respect from others that we seek.

5. *Self-actualization needs*—This is the highest level, at which we realize our full potential.

It's important to remember that Maslow's pyramid is never scaled. We don't address our physiological needs just once in our lives and never go back to that level. We address all of these challenges continuously. I think we can all agree that it's extremely hard to concentrate on anything else when the bathroom is calling or we are hungry. We must always meet our basic needs first. Until we do, nothing else matters—and we can't address all of our needs at the same time.

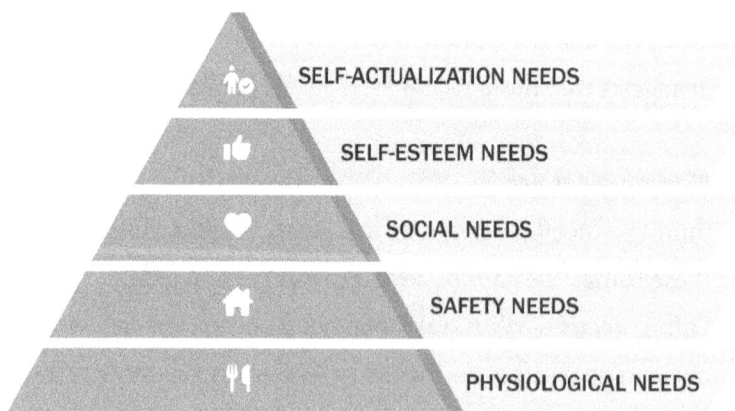

Figure 2: Maslow's Hierarchy of Needs

The same applies to the Investor Priority Pyramid (IPP), which I built for this book. The IPP is adapted from the Business Priority Pyramid developed by Mike Michalowicz and discussed in *Fix This Next*.

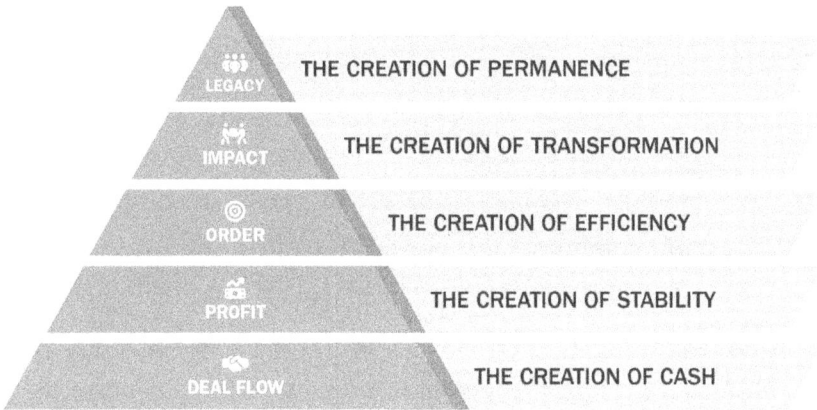

LEGACY — THE CREATION OF PERMANENCE

IMPACT — THE CREATION OF TRANSFORMATION

ORDER — THE CREATION OF EFFICIENCY

PROFIT — THE CREATION OF STABILITY

DEAL FLOW — THE CREATION OF CASH

Figure 3: The Investor Priority Pyramid (IPP)

In real estate investing, we also have a hierarchy of needs that must be addressed before we can move on. We can't build up our businesses until its basic needs are met. In real estate, these essential needs include items such as capital, properties, and sales. Without these core needs taken care of, we can't focus on other things in the business.

Just as Maslow's theory has five levels of needs, so does the IPP. The IPP levels are:

1. **Deal Flow**—This is our base level. It represents our ability to attract and deploy the cash in the business. Our business cannot survive without cash flowing into it.

2. **Profit**—At this level, our priority is retaining the cash that flows into the business. This is where our personal cash flow will be generated. We must be profitable to pay ourselves and replace our income—which requires that we master the Deal Flow level first.

3. **Order**—At this level, we are focused on maximizing efficiency and can address our scaling goals while retaining our profit and sales.

4. **Impact**—At this level, we are able to address the needs of others. We can help our team members change their situations. We can help our communities in ways that far exceed what we could have done if we tried to do it at an earlier stage.

5. **Legacy**—Finally, at this level, we can address the longevity of our business. We look at it from a long-term perspective, not trying to determine our exit strategy. Can the business we started and grew pass to another generation? How can we operate as its steward?

It's important to emphasize, again, that the levels of the IPP are not designed to be scaled. Today you might be at the Order level, focused on building efficiency, whereas tomorrow you might have to concentrate on the base level of Deal Flow—just as, in life, you must constantly tend to your most basic needs. The IPP requires constant checking and confirming of our business needs.

As I write this, it has become apparent to my management team that we have an issue with our sales team. That's a lower-level issue, which means my attention is needed there before I get to Order-level issues. Just as there is no shame in getting up each day needing to eat, a base-level activity, there is no shame in needing to address a lower-level need in your business.

THE IPP'S CORE NEEDS

WITHIN EACH OF THE IPP's five fundamental needs are five core needs. The core needs are the needs within each fundamental level that the business must master to function and grow at that level. The core needs are listed below. This may seem like a lot, but don't worry; we will fully explore each core need in Chapters 3-8.

Foundation Level: Deal Flow

1. *Lifestyle Congruence*—Do you know what the company's sales performance must be to support your personal comfort?
2. *Available Capital*—Do you have the capital you need to complete your next transaction?
3. *Deal Attraction*—Do you have enough deal flow to support your acquisition target goals?
4. *Prospect Attraction*—Do you attract enough quality prospects to support your needed sales?
5. *Client Conversion*—Do you convert enough of the right prospects into clients to support your needed sales?

Foundation Level: Profit

1. *Debt Eradication*—Do you consistently remove debt rather than accumulate it?
2. *Profitable Leverage*—When debt is used, is it to generate predictable, increased profitability?
3. *Margin Health*—Do you have healthy profits within each of your offerings, and do you continually seek ways to increase them?

4. *Transaction Frequency*—Do you maximize your revenue from each client?

5. *Cash Reserves*—Does the business have enough cash reserves to cover all expenses for three months or longer?

Foundation Level: Order

1. *Minimized Wasted Effort*—Do you have an ongoing, working model that helps you reduce bottlenecks, slowdowns, and inefficiencies?

2. *Role Alignment*—Are people's roles and responsibilities matched to their talents?

3. *Outcome Delegation*—Are the people closest to the problem empowered to resolve it?

4. *Linchpin Redundancy*—Is your business designed to operate unabated when key employees are unavailable?

5. *Mastery Reputation*—Are you known in your industry for being the best at what you do?

Foundation Level: Impact

1. *Transformation Orientation*—Does your business benefit clients through a transformation beyond the transaction?

2. *Mission Motivation*—Are all employees (including leadership) motivated more by delivering on the mission than by their individual roles?

3. *Dream Alignment*—Are employees' individual dreams aligned with the business's grand vision?

4. *Feedback Integrity*—Are your people, clients, and community empowered to give both critical and complimentary feedback?

5. *Complementary Network*—Does your business seek to collaborate with vendors (including competitors) who serve the same customer base to improve the customer experience?

Foundation Level: Legacy

1. *Intentional Leadership Turn*—Is there a plan for leadership to transition and stay fresh?

2. *Quarterly Dynamics*—Does your business have a clear vision for its future and dynamically adjust on a quarterly basis to bring that vision to fruition?

3. *Ongoing Adaptation*—Is the business designed to constantly adapt and improve, including finding ways to better and beat itself?

4. *Client Cooperation*—Do you foster cooperation with and support for your clients in need?

5. *Legacy of Contribution*—Is the organization's impact recognized and amplified by individuals and organizations aligned with its values?

After reviewing the core needs above, you might be thinking, *Wait, my business is special, I have a core need that's not listed.* I hear you. Just as human DNA is 99.9% the same, businesses might have differences but operate with many core similarities. Later, I will address how you can further modify each fundamental level and add your own core needs if you feel it is necessary. For now, keep reading, learn how to apply the IPP to your business, and you will have the framework you need to grow it.

THE IPP HELPED ME ACHIEVE MY DREAMS

AFTER I FINISHED MY WALK in the park, I got into my car with its nice cold air conditioning and went to one of my favorite Oklahoma City restaurants, Toby Keith's I Love this Bar. Yep, that's the name of the restaurant, and it's not a bar. I took my trusty notepad inside and began to create a current process map showing how my real estate investment company operated. In between bites of country fried steak smothered in gravy, I documented each step of how work flowed through my business. I started at the very beginning, with mailing, and delineated the whole process through the end of a hypothetical transaction. I now refer to this as swimlaning, and I use it in teaching.

I turned my notepad horizontally and drew four lines across the paper, creating what looked like swimmers' lanes at a swim meet. Each lane was dedicated to a person or process—the actors. On the left side of each lane, I listed the actors who supported that lane:

- Me in the top lane
- My Virtual Assistant in the second lane
- Technology in the third lane
- And finally, in the fourth lane, external parties in the transaction like the seller, the county, brokers, and others outside my company.

After I had the paper set up, I started at the beginning of a process and mapped out each step. If I performed the task, it was in my lane.

If a VA performed a task, it was in the VA lane. Step by step, I mapped out the process and how the work flowed between people and lanes.

This exercise can help you identify bottlenecks in your workflows. If you want to give it a try, check out the video example of this concept on the FTNREI resources page:

www.FixThisNextForRealEstateInvestors.com

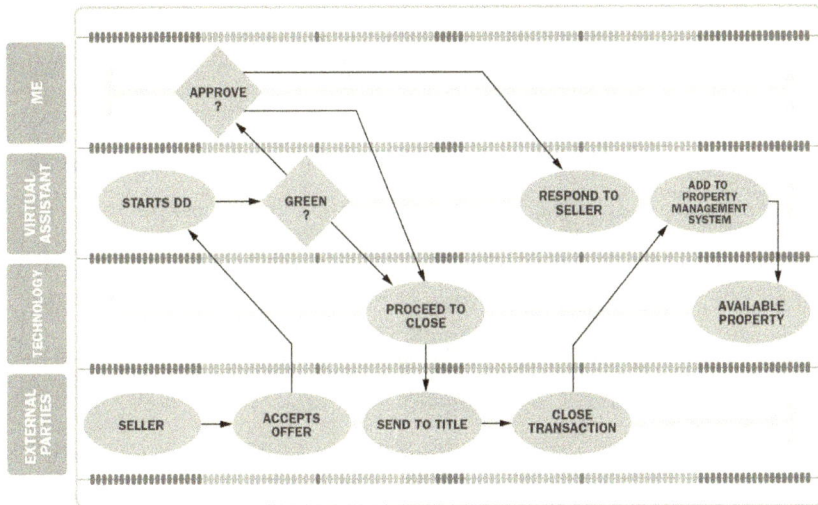

Figure 4: Swimlane Example

The energy of the restaurant had me in a zone. I was meticulous in my mapping. At the end, I had an entire view of how my business operated.

Back in my hotel room, I sat at the desk and admired my work. I felt like a football coach holding a big chart of all the game plays. This was my playbook. As I scanned every function, it hit me; the problem was revealed, and I could see the weakest link. I realized in that instant that if I fixed that one thing, deals could move through my system much faster.

The problem was me; almost every step relied on me. I was the linchpin of the business. I was trying to do everything, so it was only growing to my capacity. You may have heard that a fish's size is limited by the size of its space. The same is true for your business. If you expand the capacity of the tank, your fish will grow larger. If you expand the capacity of your team, your company will grow.

If the Investor's Priority Pyramid had existed in 2015, I would have identified my fundamental need as the Order level. Yep, I was in the third level of what today is the IPP. My next action was to add team members to alleviate the constraint of my time. Hiring people created new challenges and changed my fundamental need. After I started building the team, my core need changed and I now had a Deal Flow-level need. See how one change in my business resulted in a change to my fundamental need level? From this point on, I constantly shifted my focus to prioritize what it needed most.

As I solved the most pressing issues, my monthly income grew more and more quickly. In 2015, the business grew ten times. I admit that the starting number was small, but 1,000% revenue growth in one year is quite remarkable. The business continued to grow as 2016 began. And then it happened—layoff day.

On February 10, 2016, the senior IT leaders at my corporate job announced that they were outsourcing 85% of the 500-member team. But I was prepared because I was already following a systematic method that kept me moving toward my goal of replacing my income and realizing the joys of working for myself.

I want this for you, too. It pains me to recall Jonathan's story, which I shared in the introduction, and the countless similar stories I've heard. I want everyone who chooses real estate as their investment model to achieve their dreams. I want you to have the time, money, and freedom you desire. And I know that as you learn and apply the IPP to your business, it will serve as the compass that guides you toward that life of freedom.

THE IPP IS A TOOL FOR YOU AND YOUR TEAM

THE USEFULNESS OF THE IPP and this book are not limited to just you. I designed them so that you and your team have a common framework to guide you to the next issue.

As I write this, my hometown has just been hit by a hurricane. It was a major storm and the devastation to homes and property was monumental. The impact for me and my family was damage to our roof, but also a loss of power for sixty-seven hours. Imagine the job facing the power company when 70% of all customers in the Tampa area lost their power. How do you go about restoring power when such a large portion of the customer base is affected? The power company began by following a very methodical process. They started with over 600,000 customers out of power; within one week, it was down to less than 30,000.

Watching the restoration unfold after the storm was incredible. First, the power company recruited 6,000 additional linemen, who started at the power plants and worked outward through the system, first addressing issues that prevented the power from arriving at the substations. Then they began working on the substations. With the substations back online, they started to repair the power lines. Working together, they moved from one problem to the next until everyone's power was restored.

The IPP is just like that. You could work it on your own, but keeping this framework to yourself slows your progress. Having team members who understand the Fix This Next for Real Estate Investors framework and the IPP gives you both speed and a common language.

Share the Fix This Next resources on www.FixThisNextForReal EstateInvestors.com so they understand how the process works.. Have them complete the IPP assessments with you. Doing this will allow you to have more eyes on both current issues and potential ones.

Finally, the more people you share this framework with, the less dependent your business will be on you. Isn't that the dream?

COMMITMENT TIME

ARE YOU WITH ME? ARE you ready to commit to learning the IPP and applying it to your business? I hope so! Here's your first step: Send a commitment email to Scott@ScottTodd.net and type "IPP Commitment" in the subject line so I can find your email in my ever-growing inbox.

Chapter 2

FIND IT
AND FIX IT

YOU ARE A PROBLEM-SOLVER, AND SO ARE THE TEAM MEMBERS who work with you. Real estate investing is nothing more than solving problems. When you buy a property, you work with the seller to identify what issue they want to address and then structure the deal to create a winning solution for both you and the seller. When you partner with investors, the challenge is to put their idle capital to work in a way that rewards both them and you. When you sell a property, you try to understand the buyer's goals so you can—you guessed it—address their problem.

The advantage of being a problem-solver is that your brain is consistently trying to identify and solve problems. These might be real challenges in your business or potential future ones that never manifest; either way, you are on alert and won't let anything slip by you.

The flip side is that your brain is also trying to solve as many problems as possible. The brain is a high-speed computer processor that diligently works to identify and surmount as many obstacles as it can, as quickly as it can.

And there's the rub: You can't possibly fix everything at one time. It's impossible. And when we attempt to do too many things at once, we fail. Just as a computer blue-screens when it has memory overload, we too can become overwhelmed and freeze up.

You and your team can only prioritize one major issue at a time. You can't concentrate on building efficiencies, for example, when you are struggling to raise capital. The goal is to identify the weakest link and fix it.

YOUR WEAKEST LINKS DEFINE YOUR LIMITS

As ELI GOLDRATT DISCUSSES IN his must-read book, *The Goal*, the theory of constraints (TOC) applies to all businesses.[7] It is based on the principle that a system is only as strong as its weakest link. When we strengthen or fix the weakest link, we greatly improve the ability of the system to perform closer to maximum performance. However, fixing one weak link moves us to the next weakest link. Chasing these down can sometimes feel like playing a game of Whac-a-Mole. You must have the resolve to persevere until all the weak links are fixed or gone.

In Chapter 1, I shared my Oklahoma City story and my realization that I had become the linchpin of the business, meaning I was the weakest link. I had maxed out my company's ability to grow because it was just me and one virtual assistant. I needed more help—thus my state of overwhelm.

Your team members may feel overwhelmed, too, but do they have permission to tell you? I address that in a later chapter.

BUSINESSES ARE COLLECTIONS OF SYSTEMS

EVERY BUSINESS IS A COLLECTION of systems, from property acquisition to due diligence to marketing and accounting. Real estate is a system; even a single house is a collection of structural systems, HVAC systems, plumbing systems, and so on. The theory of constraints applies to all systems. We must identify the weakest link first, fix it, and then move on to the next weakest link.

Consider a house with a leaky roof and a kitchen that needs new cabinets. Is your first priority getting the cabinets installed or the roof fixed? I think we can agree that the roof contractor is probably our first call, even if you are a member of the multitasking investors club and your answer is "I'd call both because it'll take some time to get the cabinets installed." You still have to choose one call to make first, and I bet it's the roofer.

Our job is simple: to find the most pressing issue or weakest link, not by following our gut but by using our framework, supported by data. Just like a pilot who enters IMC, we know that we can't trust our instincts, we must follow our instruments.

And if you hate data and want to make decisions based on instinct, maybe you should consider the Jerry Seinfeld Method. If you are unfamiliar with Seinfeld, he's a comedian and one of the main characters in the TV sitcom *Seinfeld*. In one episode, Seinfeld declares, "If every instinct you have is wrong, doing the opposite must be right."[8]

THE SCALING TRAP

I HEAR THE WORD "SCALE" all the time. It's a great buzzword. "How do I scale my business?" Wanting to scale your company is great; the trouble is that most people try to scale in the wrong sequence, which is like trying to make their business run before it can walk.

You need a strong infrastructure in place before you can scale. By infrastructure, I mean the systems within the business. For example, you can't scale if you don't have a repeatable capital attraction system. If you consistently struggle to raise capital, that is a weak link to strengthen before you attempt to scale.

Imagine you were building a home. A plumber would not install the lines, tell you to put up the drywall, and then turn on the water. They would first run a pressure test to look for leaks and potential weaknesses in the system. If any were found, they would fix the weakest link—improperly fitted pipes—and run the test again. After they completed the test runs, they could turn the water on at full pressure with confidence and you could go ahead and construct your walls.

Trying to scale too soon can serve as a blow to your confidence and be detrimental to your long-term success. Scaling requires you to take a methodical approach to tackling one vital need at a time until your business can handle more volume.

It's time to make progress. You and your team will follow a four-step process:

1. Identify the needs of the business.
2. Find the vital need.
3. Fix it.
4. Repeat.

You will work this process again and again to achieve your goals and build the company of your dreams.

IDENTIFYING THE NEEDS OF THE BUSINESS

ALL BUSINESSES HAVE MULTIPLE COMPETING needs. The first need you have to manage is your own. I know you feel an urge to try to fix as many things as you can right now, but remember, you can't. Remind your problem-solving self that you are building a solid foundation, and you do that one step at a time. You will strengthen all the weak links, but you have to do it one link at a time. At times this can feel overwhelming, given everything that needs to be done. You want the end results sooner. But rushing it never works.

All problems and tasks can easily be sorted to help you zero in on the one thing you need to do next. Often, addressing this one big thing will catapult you toward the next most important issue. Fixing one thing will result in the exposure of your next weakest link.

Your business has fundamental needs, core needs, and one vital need.

As I shared in Chapter 1, the five fundamental needs of the IPP are Deal Flow, Profit, Order, Impact, and Legacy. Each level of fundamental need contains five potential core needs. Each core need has an associated question that you should answer. Your answer to each question will either be yes or no. If you are unsure, treat that as a no.

Your no answers help you identify the core needs you need to address in order for your business to grow and scale.

FIND THE VITAL NEED

Although your business can have several core needs, only one can be considered its vital need. The vital need is the one thing you need to fix right now to move on to the next level. Remember the leaky roof and the cabinets. Who should you call first?

To identify your vital need, look at the questions you answered no to in the assessment. These point to your core needs. Then, find the one that sits at the lowest foundational level. That's your vital need.

Figure 5 shows part of a completed IPP. You will see two questions with no answers. Because Available Capital and Prospect Attraction are marked no, they are core needs. However, because we can't serve multiple needs at once, we need to default to the vital need. In this case, the vital need is Available Capital. This is the vital need because it is closer to the bottom in the hierarchy of needs. Working on this need first will give the business the biggest boost. This is the one thing we need to fix now.

DEAL FLOW / SALES

Lifestyle Congruence

Do you know what the company's sales performance must be to support your personal comfort?   ☑ Yes ☐ No

Available Capital

Do you have the needed capital to complete your next transaction?   ☐ Yes ☑ No ◀—— VITAL NEED

Each no answer is a **core** need.

Deal Attraction

Do you have enough deal flow to support your acquisition target goals?   ☑ Yes ☐ No

The lowest no is your **vital** need.

Prospect Attraction

Do you attract enough quality prospects to support your needed sales?   ☐ Yes ☑ No ◀—— CORE NEED

Client Conversion

Do you convert enough of the right prospects into clients to support your needed sales?   ☑ Yes ☐ No

Figure 5: Sample Completed IPP

I provide another example in Figure 6. In this example, all the Deal Flow needs have yes answers, so that level is met for now. However, in the Profit level, three core needs exist: Transaction Frequency, Margin Health, and Cash Reserves. Because Transaction Frequency is a lower-level need, it becomes the vital need. After addressing it, we move on to the next vital need.

The IPP keeps our attention on the most important business need. You'll find that when you and your team consistently do that, you will resolve each issue more quickly.

DEAL FLOW / SALES

Lifestyle Congruence

Do you know what the company's sales performance must be to support your personal comfort? ☑ Yes ☐ No

Available Capital

Do you have the needed capital to complete your next transaction? ☑ Yes ☐ No

Deal Attraction

Do you have enough deal flow to support your acquisition target goals? ☑ Yes ☐ No

Prospect Attraction

Do you attract enough quality prospects to support your needed sales? ☑ Yes ☐ No

Client Conversion

Do you convert enough of the right prospects into clients to support your needed sales? ☑ Yes ☐ No

Each no answer is a **core** need.

The lowest no is your **vital** need.

PROFIT			
Debt Eradication			Each no answer is a **core** need.
Do you consistently remove debt rather than accumulate it?	☑ Yes ☐ No		
			The lowest no is your **vital** need.
Profitable Leverage			
When debt is used, is it to generate predictable, increased profitability?	☑ Yes ☐ No		
Transaction Frequency			
Do you maximize your revenue from each client?	☐ Yes ☑ No	◄——— VITAL NEED	
Margin Health			
Do you have healthy profits within each of your offerings, and do you continually seek ways to increase them?	☐ Yes ☑ No	◄——— CORE NEED	
Cash Reserves			
Does the business have enough cash reserves to cover all expenses for three months or longer?	☐ Yes ☑ No	◄——— CORE NEED	

Figure 6: Sample Completed IPP #2

At the end of this chapter, I ask you to complete the IPP assessment. For now, let's keep learning the FTN process.

FIX IT

FIXING THE ISSUES IS WHERE the fun begins. After you have identified your vital need, it's time to brainstorm, question-storm, problem-solve, or empower the process improvement team. Whatever method you prefer, now is the time to gather the team and work through possible solutions. This is the time to strengthen or replace that weak link.

Begin with a strong problem statement. Research has shown that there are five parts to a well-structured one:

1. The statement references something that the organization cares about and connects that element to a clear and specific goal.
2. The statement contains a clear articulation of the gap between the current state and the goal.
3. The target you are trying to accomplish, the current state, and the gap are all quantified in the statement.
4. The problem you are trying to solve is significantly small in scope and something you can tackle quickly.
5. The statement is written in a neutral manner concerning the possible root cause and the solution.

Let's practice with an example. Say our sales team uses data from our property management system when they talk with prospective buyers. One of the common issues the sales team articulates is that many records contained partial information, so they often have to stop the sales process to look up the information, and then get back to the customer. As you can imagine, slowing the sales process does not make for a great system. This presents our problem. Walking through the steps of a well-structured problem statement above, here's what we can do:

1. Reference something the organization cares about: We aim to have all records in our property management system contain complete property details.

2. Identify the gap: Currently, most property records in our property management system do not contain all the property data.

3. Target: We aim for all our records to be complete and through.

4. Small in scope: We need to review the 300 records with incomplete data, understand why the data is missing, and complete the review within thirty days.

5. Written neutrally: Notice the above words do not reference a root cause.

Our completed problem statement becomes:

"We aim to have all properties in our property management system contain complete property details. Currently, more than 50% of property records in our property management system do not contain all the property data. We aim for all our records to be complete and thorough. We need to review the 300 records with incomplete and missing data, understand why the data is missing, and complete the review within thirty days."

This strong problem statement aligns the team with the goal and the current state, and the project is doable in a short time. Make sure that these projects can be completed in ninety days or less.

You might be thinking, *What if it takes longer to fix this vital need issue?* You might need to create multiple problem statements to help you resolve it. Let's say you identify Deal Attraction as a vital need; there may be multiple problems with your sourcing of deals. For example, you may have both a pricing problem and a systemic problem with the consistency of your direct mail offers. Each of these requires its own problem statement.

THE BUSINESS KEEPS MOVING

HERE'S WHERE THE PROBLEM-SOLVERS REJOICE: We get to fix the problem while simultaneously keeping the business running. As Wharton professor Ethan Mollick explains, "Building a company is like building an airplane in flight. You are in the air seven miles up and you're trying desperately to get the engines on and put the seats in place all while at the huge risk of failing."[9]

We can't stop everything else while we are working on this problem. We can't press a pause button in business; our customers, partners, and investors need us to continue operating at our current levels. Solving this vital need should be priority number one, though, which means we shouldn't put resources toward new projects or efforts until this one is resolved.

Our job during this phase is to find the root cause of the issue. What is its source? Getting to this can be a challenge.

I'm frequently asked, "How do I know we got it?"

Identifying the real problem and doing the work to fix it might take multiple attempts. You have to establish the metrics you will use to track results and then monitor your progress. We will discuss the ACRE system that you can use for this later. For now, it's important to understand that you might not get it right the first time. You might also find that even though a fix seemed to work, it later becomes clear that the problem is not yet resolved.

There's an Old English epic poem titled *Beowulf* that I often think of when I discuss resolving root causes.

The central scene in *Beowulf* is set in a mead hall called Heorot. King Hrothgar of the Danes built Heorot, and for twelve years, a swamp monster named Grendel has terrorized the hall.

With his hall under attack, King Hrothgar requests the aid of a hero. Having heard this, Beowulf and his men arrive at Heorot ready for battle and prepared to save the hall. On the night of his arrival, Beowulf, the hero, waits for Grendel to return.

When Grendel appears, Beowulf springs into action and attacks Grendel. Grendel and Beowulf engage in an epic fight that results in Grendel losing his arm. Grendel retreats and dies from his injury.

King Hrothgar and the Danes celebrate Beowulf's victory. For saving Heorot, Beowulf and his men are honored and rewarded as the king promised.

Shortly after the celebration, there is another attack on the hall. Surprised because he had believed he killed the monster, Beowulf discovers that the attacker is none other than Grendel's mother, seeking revenge for Grendel's death.

Realizing that he still has work to do, Beowulf dives deep into the lake where Grendel's mother lives. When he finds her, he engages in yet another epic battle. As we expect, being the hero, he wins the battle and she dies. The victory again brings peace to Heorot.

Just as Beowulf believed he had found the root cause—Grendel—only to find out later that he hadn't, we too can face this reality. At times, we may have to dive deep into a situation to confront the monster's mother. This is hard work that most organizations don't do.

But once you truly confront the monster's mother, the FTN process and your business become much stronger. Talk about fixing the weak links!

SOLVING THE WRONG PROBLEM

EDWARD WILSON, AN INVESTOR WHO specializes in buy-and-hold residential properties, started laughing when I told him about watching out for Grendel's mother.

I asked, "What's so funny?"

Edward told me about one of his investing experiences from 2010. Shortly after the housing crisis began in 2008, the city of Detroit fell on even harder times. The city had been struggling for years, both financially and with a steady decline in population.

In 2009, Detroit faced a gloomy future. Two of its three auto manufacturers filed for bankruptcy protection, causing car manufacturing plants to shut down and the loss of thousands of jobs. With less demand for cars, workers in Detroit lost even more jobs. But the city's troubles started decades earlier, when families left metropolitan Detroit for the suburbs.

In 1953, former Senator and presidential candidate Mitt Romney's family sold their 5,500 square-foot home in Detroit and joined the exodus to the suburbs. In 2002, that home sold for $645,000, but it later fell into disrepair after several sequential foreclosures. By 2010, the home was abandoned and slated to be knocked down by the new mayor of Detroit, Dave Bing. The mayor had inherited a city full of vacant and abandoned homes, and to resolve the problem, he pledged to knock down 10,000 structures during his first term as mayor, including the former Romney home.

With nearly 30% of the homes in the city vacant or abandoned, housing prices declined as much as 50%.[10] Looking back today, it's easy to see that there was an oversupply of homes in the city. However, during this time, there was a lot of discussion in Edward's network about opportunities to pick up cheap houses in Detroit. Edward's plan was to purchase some of these homes, renovate them, and then rent or sell them.

Edward told me that at the time, he believed the major problem with Detroit housing was a lack of available capital to renovate these homes. He justified his investment by saying, "Detroit's a big city with a population that needs a place to live, right?"

Edward and many other investors later determined that the root cause of the housing crisis in Detroit was not a lack of capital; investors had the capital to support the renovation and repair of the homes. The central issue was the city's declining population. "Build it and they will come" didn't work. Reflecting on his experience, Edward told me that had he completed the IPP in 2010, he would have identified a Prospect Attraction need. With the houses he'd bought sitting vacant hundreds of miles away from where he lived, he thought he had a sales problem. But it wasn't until later that he realized his investment thesis had been wrong. "I didn't have a prospect attraction problem, I had a deal attraction problem. I pursued the wrong type of property," he said.

These are lessons learned, and as long as a bad deal doesn't knock you out of the game, you stand up, dust yourself off, and jump back into the swamp to look for Grendel's mother.

REPEAT

AFTER YOU RESOLVE YOUR VITAL need, it's time to redo the IPP assessment. Fixing one thing might lead to an issue in another area. Sometimes, fixing a lower-level problem might also resolve a higher-level one. The IPP will help you identify the next vital need.

This is not a task for the investor or leader only. I encourage you and each person on your team to complete an IPP assessment individually and then compare results. We often see different problems based on where we sit in the company hierarchy.

It's been said before but I'll say it again: Don't think of the IPP as scalable. Meaning that, if you are at the Order level today and you take the IPP assessment and it points to a Deal Flow-level need, you did not move backward. You are making progress; your business just needs to address a lower-level need.

To illustrate, as I write this sentence, which our friend Maslow would classify as meeting self-actualization needs (level five—the highest level) or self-esteem needs (level four), I'm getting hungry. Hunger is a physiological need (level one). Am I upset that I moved from level four or five to level one? No way! It's just how we operate as humans, and how our businesses operate.

If you look at the IPP and see that a core need listed there doesn't apply, it's OK to skip or remove it. You can refine the IPP to suit the needs of your business. Let's say you are a house flipper. Looking at the Deal Flow core needs, you feel confident that you don't have to worry about Prospect Attraction and Client Conversion because you sell everything through a realtor. Great, you can remove those two needs from the IPP. But maybe you need to add a core need such as Renovation, so you swap it for Prospect Attraction.

And if you do customize the IPP to a version that works for you, it doesn't need to have five core issues in each level. Some levels might have more, or less.

I'm often asked which core need in the IPP addresses adding people to the team. Potentially, this is in every core need. If you are working on your vital need and determine that the root cause of the problem is a lack of knowledge or lack of capacity and the solution is a person, you should consider adding a team member.

Lack of knowledge becomes a problem when you or your team don't know how to do something that needs to be done. Let's say you determine that your vital need is Client Conversion. After brainstorming with the team, you determine that the root cause is that no one in the group knows how to sell. You have two options: go down the rabbit hole of trying to learn to sell or find a capable salesperson to increase your sales. When the solution to the root cause takes you outside of your zone of experience, it's time to consider adding to the team.

Another time to consider that is when you lack capacity. This occurs when you and your team can't keep up with the work. Business comes in, but it's bottlenecked because there aren't enough people to move it through the system rapidly enough. Years ago, my company had an issue where our due diligence team regularly missed our expected turnaround time. There were always times when abnormal spikes in volume created a bottleneck in that area. But then we noticed that our overall volume had increased. Measuring the team's volume told us when we were facing a lack-of-capacity situation.

FORGET OKRS—WE USE ACRE

When I was a sophomore in college, I took a job at a computer consulting business owned by a guy named Louis. I had known Louis for four years when he hired me to work in and run his company. It was small; I was the consultant, the bookkeeper, the everything. Louis had a full-time job at the phone company, too, and his business was run by one college student at a time.

Having had a few college business classes, I was pretty sure I would crush this business and take it to a whole 'nother level. I was a fountain of ideas, and I shared each one of them with Louis. I wanted to get something going so the company could make more money and hopefully I could, too.

Louis was the type of guy who would let you go down a rabbit hole just to teach you a lesson, even if he knew you would end up looking stupid. He was the business version of Mr. Miyagi from the movie *The Karate Kid*.

I learned one of these hard-earned lessons when he allowed me to arrange a training for our customers. One of the products we supported was an accounting system. We had forty customers sign up for this training, each paying $100. My deal with Louis was that I would get 25% of the profit for teaching the class. I was so excited because we anticipated earning a profit of $3,000. My calculator showed that my pay for the event would be $750, and with Christmas coming up, I needed it. This was primarily why I had created the program.

I started the class and proceeded through my material. "This is a debit." "This is a credit." "This is a profit and loss statement."

I could feel that something was off. After I'd been teaching for about thirty minutes, one of the attendees spoke up and declared, "We know all this, it's what we do every day."

As I stood there at the front of the room, my heart dropped and I started to sweat. I glanced at Louis and he gave me that smile I had seen so many times, that *gotcha* smile. He had known for weeks that this would be a train wreck and now he was here to witness it firsthand. Quick on my feet, I replied, "I understand, I just want to make sure we are all on the same page." I didn't have a clue what to do next, because everything I had planned on teaching was just that, basic material. That was the day I learned the key rule of presenting: Know your audience.

Thankfully, I decided to pivot and start showing everyone some of the more advanced aspects of the accounting software. At the end of the class, the vocal attendee who had called me out approached me and said she was glad she had come. The event was saved, but after the workshop ended came Louis's lesson.

All of his lessons started the same way, with him addressing me very formally as "Mr. Todd." The effect was similar to your parents calling you by your full name; you knew you were in trouble.

Louis asked me what the objective of our company was. I said it was to make money. While he agreed with that premise, he explained that our real objective was to create value for our customers.

He then asked, "How do we create value for our customer?"

"To solve our customers' problems?" I asked.

He explained that in his view, the company currently had no goals; it was steering rudderless and just barely surviving. I was the second college student he had hired and given a blank canvas to create a stronger company. The first, Paul, had expanded its scope from selling and supporting software to also providing hardware sales and support contracts. "How are you going to expand the business?" he asked.

"Let's learn from this training session, get better, and start offering training sessions on the software we support," I replied.

Louis agreed and then proceeded to teach me what he knew about Peter Drucker's management by objectives (MBO) system, which Drucker discusses in his book *The Practice of Management*.[11] The first step of the MBO is to review organizational goals. Prior to our sitting down, I didn't think we had a real goal except to make money. As Louis and I went through each of the MBO steps, I could see how lacking a management framework would cause an organization to stall.

When you have a plan, a direction, it's like being on a cruise ship. Standing on deck with the wind flowing through your hair—or around your hat, in my case—the movement of the air tells you that you are heading somewhere. The same applies to a company. When you have a goal, a direction you are moving toward, you and your team can feel that movement, that energy, and things start to happen. When a company has no direction or plan, there is no breeze, no movement, and the life of the business can feel stale.

In my last corporate job, the CEO (who resigned for personal reasons) had a plan. Actually, he had too many plans. While he was still at the company, you could feel the movement. The day the new CEO started, he canceled all those projects. It felt like the ship slowed to a stop right in the middle of the sea. Not only was there was no breeze, there was also an instant fear of what would happen next.

So many businesses operate without clear goals and lack strategic direction as a result. This issue isn't confined to small companies; large ones face the same challenges.

When Andy Grove joined Intel in the mid-70s, it was at a critical juncture due to a growing number of competitors who offered products similar to Intel's, but at lower prices. The new competition came from Japanese manufacturers who began to ramp up production of DRAM (dynamic random-access memory) chips. Intel made its profit primarily from these chips, and it was under attack. DRAM chips were becoming a commodity, and we all know what happens to the profitability of commodity products: their margins become very thin.

As the new CEO, one of Grove's first challenges was to figure out how to handle the increasing competition and pricing pressures. He quickly realized that Intel lacked a framework that drove its organizational focus. To fix this, Grove developed the objectives and key results (OKR) framework. This framework gave the organization and its employees a way to identify objectives that would help pivot the company and fight off the pricing pressures it faced.

The implementation of the OKR system by Intel was key to its pivot from DRAM production to the microprocessor market, which it has now owned for years. Today, the OKR framework is used by countless organizations, including major companies like Google, Amazon, and Meta.[12]

We can't wander aimlessly toward our goals; we need a framework to help guide us. I encourage you to consider the ACRE system:

A. Articulate the objective: Determine what you want. What goal are you trying to achieve?

C. Collect the metrics you will use: Determine how you will measure success.

R. Rhythm: Next, decide how often you will review the metrics to make sure you are on track.

E. Evolve the strategy, objective, or measurement: Adjust your strategy if needed. Perhaps a different metric would work better. Maybe your rhythm is off and you're waiting too long or too short a time to monitor results. Maybe you don't need to make any adjustments at all, but if you do, this is when to do it.

Starting in Chapter 3, I do a deep dive into each of the twenty-five core needs of the IPP and apply the ACRE system to some hypothetical situations so you can gain a better understanding of how to use it to identify goals and measure your progress.

ACTION TIME

IT'S TIME TO TAKE ACTION. You are ready to complete your first IPP assessment. The process is simple; review the list of questions in Chapter 1 and answer each one. After you answer the questions, circle the core need that is at the lowest foundational level of the IPP. This becomes your vital need. This is the issue you will work on fixing next. You can also take an online assessment at www.FixThis NextForRealEstateInvestors.com.

After you have taken the assessment, read on to learn how to respond to your vital need—and all the other core needs of your business.

This book is for your entire team. At the end of most chapters, I provide a "Team Action" section where your team members can learn how to better engage with the IPP and share their feedback with you. The secret to growing your business is to get as many people helping you push the flywheel as possible. It's heavy, so let's get you some help.

TEAM ACTION: FIND IT AND FIX IT

SO MANY TIMES, IN MY work with organizations, team members are unsure of how they can contribute to growth. Let's make it a team effort. Whether you're the leader of an organization or a team member, you play an important role in helping it grow. My hope is that your whole team will join leadership and make applying the IPP framework a part of the company's culture.

If you are a team member and the leader has shared this book with you, they want your feedback. Great leaders surround themselves with talented people; you are in that group. They need your perspective because you have different strengths and see the world and the organization from a different vantage point. You provide balance. Taking the IPP assessment and being open to sharing your thoughts is vital to the long-term success of the business.

I remember a time when I saw a problem at the company where I worked and wanted to say something. I wanted to tell the vice president what I thought, but I was scared! I wrote the email, triple-checked it for errors, and then stared at the screen for hours, afraid to hit the send button. I was traveling for work, sitting in a hotel, scared to send an email. I'm not sure what I was afraid of. I guess I worried that the vice president would think I was dumb or judge me for chiming in when no one had asked for my opinion. Four hours after writing the email, I still had doubts. I called my wife and told her about it, and she asked me to read her the email. After a few more edits with her, she told me to send it. I sent the email at 10:30 p.m. Clicking "send" was probably one of the scariest moments of my professional life, but there was no going back.

As I drifted off to sleep, filled with doubt and anxiety, it was all I could think about. And when I woke up the next morning, the first thing I did I was jump on the computer to check for a response. There was nothing. The fear returned and I felt as if I had made a big mistake. Though I knew he was super busy, I wondered if the VP had read it. I wondered if he would just ignore it entirely. Around 9:30 a.m., eleven hours after I sent the email, I received a response.

"Scott, thank you for this. The feedback is well thought out, valuable, and actionable. I have forwarded it to the correct person to have them investigate it. Thanks again."

Six months later, I received a promotion.

Therefore, my advice, valued team member, is to set your doubts aside and share your opinions and thoughts. Your leadership values and needs them.

If you're not sure if what you have to say is important, I encourage you to say it anyway. Little ideas could be the start of something big.

Chapter 3

ESTABLISH PREDICTABLE DEAL FLOW

AS I WAS LEADING A BREAKOUT SESSION RECENTLY, PARTICIPANTS were sharing their current activity levels when Mitchell spoke up. "I have been at this for over year, I have purchased a few properties, but…"

I hate when success stories contain that word, "but."

He continued, "But I haven't done anything with them. I've been super busy working on building systems to support future growth. And I don't have the capital to continue."

Out of curiosity, I asked, "So did you spend all your capital on tools?"

He replied, "I have spent a lot of time and money building a custom software that will allow me to handle all my mailings and property management. The system is awesome, but I don't have the capital to buy more properties. I guess I need to focus on generating revenue from the properties I own."

This happens a lot. Instead of focusing on cash-generating activities, the oxygen of every business, it's easier to concentrate on other tasks that allow us to stay in our comfort zone. You can always tell when someone is playing it safe because they spend their time and energy on low-risk tasks like tweaking the company name or logo. These activities do not move the needle of a new company. They are not necessities.

Another example comes from a conversation I had with an investor, Daniel, when I asked him how mailing for acquisitions was going. He confessed, "I'm not mailing. I'm mapping out the entire business first so I know exactly how it will operate. Then I'll build processes and procedures so my [future] team knows how to do the work." Daniel will not need any processes unless he gets his deal flow started.

I understand Mitchell, Daniel, and the many others who follow the path of least resistance; it's easy to avoid the work that scares us. I know I'm working on important stuff when that little voice pops into my head and suggests that I go check my email or do something even less important. The significant work can easily be sidetracked by your inner critic. Prioritizing less meaningful tasks is an avoidance behavior, a form of procrastination. For me this was caused by fear, either of failure or success. We all experience some level of fear, but for most real estate investors, I see it appear mainly at the Deal Flow-level development stage.

Your business needs capital to acquire properties, and cash flow to keep it growing so you can achieve your goals. You need deal flow to keep it operational.

In real estate investing, sales can mean different things. When I refer to "sales" in this book, you should mentally replace it with whatever word or phrase signifies revenue activities in your niche.

Whether it's property sales, leasing, renting, or flipping—the specific wording is unimportant—it's about revenue. Revenue comes from having properties that create cash.

Deal Flow is the base level of the IPP because it's the core activity. It represents everything that a real estate investing company needs first to succeed and grow: cash-flowing properties. Just as Krispy Kreme Doughnuts wouldn't be a doughnut shop if it didn't have doughnuts to sell, you do not have a real estate investing business without properties that produce revenue.

Focusing on non-deal flow activities while the business needs capital and cash flow is putting the cart before the horse—and the sequence in which you address issues is important to both the sustainability of your business and its ability to help you accomplish your financial and time goals.

The rest of this chapter is designed to help you zero in on the core needs that are part of the Deal Flow fundamental level of the IPP.

NEED #1: LIFESTYLE CONGRUENCE

Question: Do you know what the company's sales performance must be to support your personal comfort?

When I still worked in my corporate job, I was driving to the office one morning when my doubts came up again. *Can I realistically replace my income?*

Our office had an open concept layout and one long desk where three or four people could work at the same time instead of cubicles. Vice presidents had offices, so I was lucky. Rolling whiteboards were positioned around the office to facilitate collaboration in the communal workspaces. You could find them near the couches or tall huddle tables and move them where they were needed. Guess where one was needed? Yep, my office.

On my way there, I noticed a whiteboard in the couch area and headed that way. With a large Diet Coke in my left hand, I grabbed the whiteboard with my right and quickly pushed it into my office. I felt guilty, as if I was in possession of contraband. As I scurried into my office, I reminded myself, *You're only plotting your exit. Clean it well when you're done, and they'll never know what you were working on!*

In my office, I closed the door, rolled my chair over to the whiteboard, and started calculating my freedom number.

The freedom number (FN) has one important job: to tell you how many deals or units it will take to generate the income you need. Here is the formula to calculate the freedom number:

FN = personal comfort number (desired monthly income) / profit margin (actual or estimated) / average revenue per unit

Knowing what your sales performance must be to support your personal comfort is the first step. We are not concerned with making millions—yet. If you are already a full-time investor, you should be concerned with the sales performance needed to support your current income. Either way, the math is the same.

After our personal expenses are satisfied, everything becomes easier. Imagine walking around with a pebble in your shoe. The pebble represents what it takes for you to live your current life. After you have enough sales to satisfy that number, the pebble disappears and walking gets a lot easier. If you are living the #vanlife and your personal comfort number is quite low, you only need a small number of sales to support it.

At this level, we are not yet concerned with profit. Profit is the next foundation level up; here we are focused specifically on what level of performance we need to sustain our lives.

That day in my office, I started by writing down the monthly income I earned from my job at the top of the whiteboard. This was my personal comfort number. I was living comfortably, and if I could generate that income from my own business, even better.

Below that, I wrote down my anticipated profit margin. Profit margin is the percentage of money left over from revenue after all the expenses are paid. Let's say that your revenue is $1,000 and your expenses total $750; that leaves a profit of $250. To calculate your profit margin, divide the profit ($250) by the revenue ($1,000). In this example, the profit margin is $250 / $1,000, or 25%. If you are already operating your business, grab the profit and loss statement and do some quick math. If you are still in the early stages and your numbers show a loss, use what you expect the profit to be after the business is stabilized.

Next, I divided my personal comfort number by my anticipated profit margin, allowing me to calculate the monthly sales performance needed to replace my income.

I then calculated how many units or properties I needed to sell to generate that amount of monthly income by taking my sales number and dividing by the average revenue per unit (door, property, and so on).

Personal Comfort Number

I need to generate $5,000 per month to be comfortable.

Profit Margin

My business generated a 25% profit margin.

Sales Performance Needed

To generate $5,000 of profit, my business needs to generate
$20,000 in revenues per month ($5,000 / 25%).

Freedom Number

I average $300 in revenue per unit. To generate $20,000 in monthly
revenue, I need sixty-seven units ($20,000 / 300).

Figure 7: Freedom Number Example

I just walked you through how to calculate your freedom number. In the ACRE section below, we will calculate a freedom number together, so keep reading. I have also created a video lesson on how to calculate your number. You can access the resources for this book at www.FixThisNextForRealEstateInvestors.com.

The math is straightforward and I could have calculated it on paper, but the whiteboard allowed me to work through other issues, such as the number of offers I would need to make and the estimated capital I would need. The process was very comforting, except that looking at what appeared to be a large sales goal seemed to make it real. Wow, that was a lot of properties I needed to acquire and sell.

After you calculate your freedom number, you know the lowest number of sales needed to support your lifestyle.

Again, I believe that you should have your entire team involved in taking the IPP assessment. This question might make you a little uncomfortable because it's about your income, but lifestyle congruence is about your business's ability to pay you, and your business needs to you to stay alive. The entire company needs this to work. If everyone else gets paid but you can't make a living, you will shut it down and move on. That would hurt your team members, who are on this journey with you. Your team needs their paychecks, and so do you.

Your personal comfort number can change, going up or down. Ideally, you will decrease your personal expenses over time and put less of a burden on your company to support you. As your income needs change, you will need to recalculate this number. If you don't know how much your business needs to generate in sales to support you and the team, fulfill this core need before addressing anything else.

I have created a Freedom Number Calculator, which is available at www.FixThisNextForRealEstateInvestors.com.

Remember: To fulfill this core need, you don't have to achieve the freedom number: You simply need to calculate what it will take for you to achieve your lifestyle.

ACRE: Lifestyle Congruence

IN CHAPTER 2, WE DISCUSSED the ACRE framework for identifying and measuring progress. At the end of each core need section, we will apply the ACRE framework to relevant examples so you can see how it works. It's time to apply ACRE to this core need.

In this ACRE example, we'll calculate the sales performance needed to support an income of $10,000 per month.

1. *Articulate the objective*: We want to generate enough income to support a $10,000-per-month personal comfort lifestyle. To

calculate this number, we'll grab our most recent profit and loss statement and calculate our profit margin. In the latest quarter, we generated $100,000 in revenue, and after expenses were paid, our profit was $30,000.

To calculate our profit margin, we take the profit of $30,000 and divide it by the revenue of $100,000; this gives us a profit margin of 30%.

Next, we need to calculate our sales performance. Because our personal comfort number is $10,000 per month, let's divide that by our profit margin of 30%, or .30.

$$\$10,000 / .30 = 30,333$$

We must generate sales of $30,333 per month to support our personal comfort level.

Now we need to calculate our revenue per unit. Let's say the average revenue per unit is $295 per month. Note that we are looking at *revenue* per unit here, not profit.

$$\$30,333 / \$295 = 112.99$$

To support our lifestyle, we need 113 units producing $295 each month.

This is our freedom number: 113 units.

2. ***Collect the metrics***: Next, let's collect the metrics we will use to measure our progress toward our freedom number. To stay motivated, we'll get a huge posterboard and a Sharpie and draw an old-school thermometer on it like the ones they use

for fundraising drives, starting with zero at the bottom and our freedom number at the top. We will slap this tracking document on the wall to serve as a constant reminder of our primary goal.

3. **Rhythm**: We want to move closer to our freedom number every month. Therefore, we'll update our tracking poster once a month. If we lose ground during the month, that's OK, it happens; we are not taking our eyes off the prize. We will proudly update our poster every month, even if the result is not what we want to see. We are on a journey and the breeze is riffling our hair.

4. **Evolve**: Our personal comfort numbers may change, and our lifestyle congruence may also change as a result. We need to be ready to recalculate our numbers. Our personal comfort number, profit margin, and revenue per unit figures are dynamic. When any of these numbers change, it's time to recalculate and then evolve our strategy as needed to support our personal comfort number.

5. **Result**: By tracking our comfort and freedom numbers, we can define success. After the target is achieved, the pebble is out of our shoe and life gets better.

NEED #2: AVAILABLE CAPITAL

Question: Do you have the capital you need to complete your next transaction?

Real estate investing is capital-intensive. Capital can come from multiple sources, ranging from your own capital to capital from investors or partners; you know, OPM (other people's money)!

The interesting thing about this core need is that it is not always present. If you are in acquisition mode, you need enough capital to fund your next deal. The key phrase here is "your next deal," not "your next ten deals."

You might be sitting there rolling your eyes and thinking, *Hey, I never need capital, I acquire properties using a low- or no-money-down strategy.* Perfect. That will work for some properties but not all. If you can consistently use that technique to acquire property, the answer to this question is yes and you can move on.

If that strategy doesn't work for you and you need capital, now is the time to get it.

Maybe you're thinking, *Wait, why does Available Capital come before Deal Attraction?* Many veteran investors love to say, "Don't worry about getting capital, find a good deal and the money will come." Maybe that's true for them, but many new investors struggle to find the capital to fund the deal they have under contract. They used their available capital as earnest money to secure the deal, performed due diligence with funds out of their own pocket, and then started the search for capital. Often, the search ends unsuccessfully before the close date expires.

I presented the Fix This Next for Real Estate Investors system at a real estate investment association (REIA) meeting. When I was done, they opened the meeting to a segment they called "Deal Funders." A new investor mustered the courage to get up in front of all these other investors and present his deal. He had secured an eight-unit, multifamily property in a nearby town. Despite his nervousness in front of what new investors might consider an intimidating crowd, his presentation was engaging and all the numbers looked good. The units needed minor updates and there were some parking lot issues, but the *pro forma* statement looked sound. He was seeking $200,000 to cover the down payment and closing cost and he needed to close in ten days. He had secured the property with $10,000 in escrow and performed due diligence. He completed his presentation and that was it. No one expressed an interest. Have you ever been to an open mic night at the comedy club where the comedian tells joke after joke and no one laughs? It was like that. I felt bad for the guy. I emailed him as I was writing this book to ask, "Did you get the funds to close that deal?"

"No," he told me. "I could not make it happen. I lost my deposit and the money I spent on due diligence."

The number one thing stopping him from acquiring the property was not deal attraction: It was a lack of capital. If you don't have the capital lined up for your next acquisition, that should be your focus.

The "Find the deal and the capital will appear" mantra only works when you have built a capital network. You won't find capital just by presenting a deal. Investors work with the operators they know and trust, and trust comes out of relationship. Capital partners want one thing: Their money back. They don't just throw it at any deal they hear about.

Maybe you're thinking, *I'm not good at raising capital, I'm an introvert and couldn't ask for it.* I hear you and I feel your pain. If asking for capital seems terrifying, remember, those investors need you. Why? Because they have capital sitting idle in the bank, barely growing. They need your deal. You need to find ways to connect with potential partners and show them that you can help solve their problem.

Real estate investor J. Massey once shared his strategy for finding capital partners: He arranged meet-ups for those seeking to learn about building cash flow in which the attendees played Robert

Kiyosaki's *Rich Dad's Cash Flow* board game. J. moderated the group as they played the game, which gave him the opportunity to get to know people who were interested in cash-flowing assets (think potential investors). Playing the game, they learned why real estate is such a great place for cash flow. Then, after the game, he was able to follow up with new potential investment partners.

As your business grows, you might bring in a capital acquisition team whose job is to acquire capital. Raising capital is not something you personally have to do forever, unless you want to.

ACRE: Available Capital

IT'S ACRE TIME, AND TIME to raise some capital to complete our next deal. We estimate that we will need $200,000 in capital to do this.

1. *Articulate the objective*: Our objective is to find four partners who will each contribute $50,000.
2. *Collect the metrics*: We know that not every potential partner we meet will be able to invest the $50,000; maybe they don't have the idle funds, or maybe it's not the right time for them. Our goal, however, is to meet as many of them as possible. We want them in our growing Rolodex. We will track our progress with qualified potential partners (QPP) to measure our success: The goal is for one out of ten QPPs to be ready to invest in our upcoming deal.
3. *Rhythm*: We commit to meeting ten new QPPs each week and targeting one REIA meeting per week. We find four REIA chapters to visit in the metro market or around the state.

4. **Evolve**: After attending two REIA meetings, we discover that we are not getting close to our goal of meeting ten new QPPs per week. It's time to evolve the strategy. This could mean reducing the QPP goal, attending more meetings, or heck, investing in some board games.

5. **Result**: Having built relationships with potential capital partners, we can look for our next acquisition knowing that the funds are available.

NEED #3: DEAL ATTRACTION

Question: Do you have enough deal flow to support your acquisition target goals?

You can't grow your investment business without adequate deal flow. In some real estate niches such as multifamily or self-storage units, it's typical to buy a property, stabilize it, and then acquire another. Maybe your target is one property per year or one per quarter. If you're not in property acquisition mode right now, this core need may not apply to you. Answer yes to this question unless you are in acquisition mode.

Other investors, such as house flippers, land investors, and wholesalers, always need property. If your system is attracting the deals you need, you too can answer yes to this question.

Being in deal attraction mode means creating a systematic process to surface the right acquisition targets. Whether your system involves mailing offer letters or other methods, consistency is important. More important, though, is the ability to attract right-fit targets. Attracting properties that don't meet your acquisition requirements wastes money and precious time. Your goal should be to attract properties that meet your requirements and that you can close.

At one point, bored with land investing and ready to expand, I started looking at investing in a mobile home park. As I began to search for properties, I noticed that I was attracting deals that did not meet my requirements. The cap rates were either too low or artificially inflated to future *pro forma* values, meaning that the sellers were trying to sell at prices that reflected improvements they hadn't actually completed. They were trying to get credit for work that I would have to do. Other deals just were not financeable. How do I know? Because I wasted time and money on due diligence and application fees seeking financing, all to no avail. There was clearly something wrong with my attraction system.

I have also run complete mailing strategies where I had to send way more offer letters to generate an accepted offer than was typical for my niche. In some mailing batches, most of the accepted offers required that the property be probated, which would have cost more than the property was worth.

There are numerous stories about house flippers who send 5,000 offer letters to get a single accepted offer. Is that good? It depends on your market or niche. In my niche of land investing, it's terrible; in others, such as house flipping, it might be a great response.

Some investors bypass the entire direct mail process and focus solely on building a network of brokers who routinely bring them off-market deals. For example, Frank Rolfe and Dave Reynolds, the fifth-largest owners of mobile home parks in the US, currently own over 2,750 mobile home parks in twenty-five states with a combined market value that exceeds $700 million. Their acquisition team has the luxury of brokers bringing them countless off-market deals. But their acquisition strategy doesn't end there; they continue to build relationships with other operators in the markets they serve. When owners decide to retire or sell, who do they call? Yep, Frank and Dave. Their relationships with brokers and other operators reflect their commitment to the long game. They aren't just focused on property acquisition today; they have built a system to sustain their deal flow for years to come.

To me, the most important rule of property acquisition is that when you commit to closing on a property, you do it. Ensuring that I close on properties on time has earned me a great reputation. This reputation has allowed me access to deals I couldn't have gotten in the early days of my investing career. A key part of your property attraction system should be to build a similar reputation. Word will spread and before you know it, deals will flow to you as if you were in possession of a giant deal magnet.

Your goal is not just to look at deals, but ones that fit your investment criteria. Attracting a consistent flow of unsuitable properties will cause you to question if your purchase criteria are wrong or impossible. Then you compromise on your investment criteria and end up in a bad deal.

Remember, you want a consistent flow of right-fit targets. You also need to quiet the fearful inner critic who creeps into your investment criteria, making them unrealistic.

Mitch Daniels, a multifamily investor, has a goal to invest in two or three eighty-to-one-hundred-unit multifamily properties per year. Mitch shared with me that nothing that was hitting his desk lately was exciting to him, and he worried that he was becoming too selective. During our discussion, he mentioned that the market cap rates had gone down and he couldn't justify investing in lower-cap-rate properties. He felt stuck.

Mitch's market changed and he held firm on his investment criteria; that's a good thing. It's smarter to pass on a deal that doesn't work than to break your investing rules and end up in a bad investment. However, I pointed out to Mitch that while his primary market was encountering pricing pressures, many other markets were not. Maybe he should shift his acquisition strategy to a new market and face less pressure as a result.

It's easy to fall into the "there are no deals in my market" trap. Maybe you only want to acquire properties in your home market. If nothing looks good right now and you want to wait, be sure you are not allowing fear to set unrealistic investment criteria.

In the years leading up to 2017, a single-family investor I know built a portfolio of 300 rental properties. In 2017, he believed that the market was peaking and began divesting himself of his units. He told me, "As I see prices peaking here in Florida, I've unloaded my rental portfolio. I started that process over a year ago. I'm about 90% divested, I've got about 10% [thirty properties] or so to go and I'm out." Fearing a peak, his strategy was to wait until the properties declined in value and reenter the market at the lower price. This strategy would create a higher net cash flow. Meanwhile, from 2017 to 2022, Zillow data suggests that the average house price increased by 54% and average rental rates also increased during this period.[13] He allowed fear of a correction to affect his investment criteria.

If your deal attraction system is not producing the flow you need, it's time to change it up. What can you do to get this area working more efficiently?

ACRE: Deal Attraction

IN THIS ACRE EXAMPLE, WE'LL create an acquisition system that allows us to track and improve our right-fit strategy.

1. ***Articulate the objective***: We want to build a deal attraction system for our multifamily operation that generates a continuous flow of properties that meet our criteria. Our strategy is a multichannel approach. First, we'll start a mailing campaign to mom-and-pop operators of twelve- to twenty-door garden apartment units. We have identified the three metro markets we are open to working in and will target them with a mailing piece that invites them to contact us to start a conversation. This business is about relationships, and our strategy is centered on developing them, so our next step will be to identify the top five brokers in the market who specialize in garden complexes. After identifying these brokers, we will start building relationships with them, giving them very clear specifications about the type of properties we're seeking. We will share our capital attraction strategy with them so they know we are serious and can close if the property is right.

Our target is to buy four units per year. Historically, we close on one property for every twenty units we review, making our close rate 5%.

2. ***Collect the metric***: With our historical close rate in mind, we know we need to get better at targeting properties. We aim to improve our close rate and bring it from 5% to 10%.

3. **Rhythm**: Because we are trying to acquire one property per quarter, we will measure our progress quarterly.

4. **Evolve**: In our first quarter, our brokers brought us zero units to review and our mailing produced five units. We closed on zero. After speaking with our broker team, we learned that our desired cap rate is a little too high. We were seeking a 10% cap, but the market is yielding 8.5-9%, so we told our brokers to adjust the strategy and bring us properties in the 8.5-9% cap range. We also adjusted our mailings. The next quarter, we looked at twelve deals and purchased one. This produced an 8% close rate, better than the baseline but still short. We will keep evolving until the target metric is achieved.

5. **Result**: We now spend less time looking at deals because we're attracting right-fit targets. We are putting that newfound time toward our next core need.

SALES

WITH OUR FREEDOM NUMBER CALCULATED, capital in place, and acquisition strategy in check, it's time to shift to the sales portion of the IPP.

If this book were a *Choose Your Own Adventure*, this would be one of those pivotal moments to decide which path to take. Earlier I mentioned that human DNA is 99.9% the same, and that is essentially true of real estate investment businesses. However, the next part of this Deal Flow base layer is sales, and developing a sales framework that supports all investors is challenging because niches operate somewhat differently. If, for example, you're a fix-and-flip investor who sells through a realtor, I suggest that you modify this foundational level to include renovations. The sales aspect of this level is likely less significant for you because the realtor handles that part of your business.

I encourage you to modify the core needs to suit your business. That's the beauty of this framework; it is flexible enough to support your specific goals and vision.

That said, let's move on—just remember that when we discuss "sales," you can mentally swap that word for lease, rent, flip, or whatever generates revenue in your real estate niche.

NEED #4: PROSPECT ATTRACTION

Question: Do you attract enough quality prospects to support your needed sales?

Who are your customers? As much as we want to believe that everyone is our customer, they aren't. In *Fix This Next,* Mike Michalowicz explains that there are three stages of awareness when it comes to finding clients: "Most business owners go through three stages of awareness when it comes to finding clients or customers. First, there is the 'anybody' stage, when you ignore your mom's warnings of 'stranger danger' and think everyone in the world is a potential client. Next, you realize you are way off base, and you choose a market to sell to.

This decision is usually based on what other businesses are doing or not doing. Finally, you find your market—a market that serves your business. To find this market, you need to be clear about what your company can do, what your company wants, and what your company needs."[14]

One of my favorite movies is *Wayne's World*. I loved that movie so much that I used a line from it to get my wife's phone number (thanks, Wayne!), but that's a story for a different day.

Wayne introduces himself to the audience using one of my favorite lines: "I've had plenty of jo-jobs; nothing I'd call a career."[15] Like Wayne, I've had plenty of jo-jobs, one of which was investment representative for a financial services firm. The job was to find people with money to invest in securities and help them invest it. When I started, I thought everyone was a prospect. That was stage-one thinking that I soon discovered is incorrect.

I started noticing a trend: retirees were very interested in bonds. They enjoyed the quarterly interest payments hitting their accounts. So I arrived at stage two, I found a market, but I still had work to do. I hadn't yet connected with these customers.

I looked at the clients I had connected with and made a list of what they had in common. There were patterns; first, a lot of them were golfers. I grew up playing golf and working at a golf course, so we shared a bond. Another trait I noticed was that a large number of these clients were women, specifically widows. I had this job when my grandfather passed and I was helping my grandmother with her finances. I believe I was able to connect with the widows because in helping them, I was helping people like my grandmother.

Narrowing down my clients was stage three. I had found my market.

All businesses struggle with this. We can't serve everyone; we must find our people.

The fast track to fulfilling this core need is to think carefully about the customers you currently serve. Let's say you have a self-storage facility. What do your tenants have in common? Are they apartment dwellers who need extra space? Are they business owners who have storage needs? Do they operate businesses from their units? To find our stage three prospects, we look at who we attract as clients and how we can serve them better.

Finding my own stage three prospects greatly increased my volume and profits. Business became a lot easier. In fact, the transformation was incredible. As a land investor, I had the entire US to choose from. There was a county I liked in Florida, about 2.5 million acres in size. Within that county, I found an area I connected with that was about 50,000 acres.

When I say I connected with the area, I mean that I connected with the market. I understood the pricing, I had my purchase price dialed in, and I understood the sellers and buyers. It took about ten months of trying out lots of different markets, but I found my people—and when the connection was made, my work became virtually frictionless.

Now it's time to find your stage three prospects. Satisfying this core need of Prospect Attraction will take some work. It might happen quickly or slowly, but your goal here is to find your people: the people you enjoy serving, the people you can talk to for hours. When you find them, your life and your team's lives get so much easier.

Most coaches and marketing experts will advise you to build a customer avatar. What do they do for work, do they live in a house, do they own or rent, and so on. All that demographic data is fine, but it's the psychographic data you need most. You want to understand the customers and the problem they are trying to solve. When you understand their psychographic profile, it becomes easier to attract more of them through your marketing.

If you don't have customers yet, or enough of them to find a pattern, start at stage two and choose your market. Then dial in your marketing, using common traits to find your people.

Again, this might take some time. At its core, prospect attraction is a marketing issue, and you may need to learn more about marketing and techniques to find solutions to this problem. You can fix it by refining your message until you find your people. Don't forget, they need you as much as you need them.

ACRE: Prospect Attraction

IN THIS SCENARIO, LET'S PUT on our land investing hats and head out to find our market.

1. *Articulate the objective*: Our objectives are to attract quality prospects who are interested in purchasing rural land and generate one hundred qualified leads per month.
2. *Collect the metric*: To measure the effectiveness of our prospect attraction strategies, we will track:
   - The number of leads generated per month by each source. The goal is one hundred leads per month, resulting in ten sales per month.
   - The engagement of our leads with our marketing material. This includes email open rates and social media interactions.
3. *Rhythm*: Because our goal is monthly, we will track our progress monthly and adjust as needed.
4. *Evolve*: The goal is simple, and the marketing team now understands how to judge success. They can look at their efforts and adjust as needed based on the number of leads they produce.

Regular team meetings and transparency around results will help the team adjust as needed.

5. **Result**: After six months of continuous improvement, the company now averages 120 leads per month with an 8% conversion rate, allowing it to achieve its goal of ten sales per month.

NEED #5: CLIENT CONVERSION

Question: Do you convert enough of the right prospects into clients to support your needed sales?

In the last core need, Prospect Attraction, we discussed finding your market. We also addressed the fact that attracting prospects is a function of marketing. This core need, Client Conversion, is about converting those prospects into clients. This is sales.

If you are generating prospects but not converting them into clients, you need to do a deep dive to understand if and how your offering solves their problems.

Here's an important question: What problem are your prospects trying to solve? We all have problems, real or perceived. We do not purchase anything unless we believe it will solve a problem in our lives. Look around you: virtually everything you own was purchased for that reason.

Three months after I was laid off, my son and I took a trip to California, where I was leading a workshop. I was newly self-employed, and we were also preparing for back-to-school season, so money was tight. As we walked down the Venice Beach Boardwalk, passing all the stores selling tchotchkes, a two-foot, branded Venice Beach surfboard caught my eye. I thought about getting it for my office as a reminder of my first trip as a self-employed dude. It was cheap, ten dollars, but I did not buy it because I knew I might need that money for school supplies or other living expenses. I didn't know what the future might hold.

I was stuck in the lowest-level need on Maslow's scale, and my priority was making sure my family's basic needs were met. One year later I was back for the same event, walking the boardwalk once again, but this time I was higher on Maslow's scale. Ten dollars for a mini surfboard was not a problem. It sits in my office to this day.

Why did I buy it? What problem does a dust-collecting mini surfboard solve? This thing solves no real problem, but it does solve a perceived one: It represents the fact that I moved past a challenging point in my life. I made it my participation trophy!

Every offering you have solves a problem for someone, though it may or may not be evident to a prospect that they have this problem.

When it's clear to them that they do, they start seeking a solution. The greater challenge comes from the prospect who doesn't realize it. Because they are unaware of the problem, they don't actively seek a solution.

You will find two types of consumers in this group. The first is truly unaware of the problem. No problem, no need for a solution. The second is those who fear addressing the problem. This fear could come from a belief that the solution is too expensive.

When you understand the problem faced by your prospect, you can start to address it with them. It can be basic, like "I need a place to live," or more complex, like "I need a place to live, but six months ago I lost my job, couldn't pay my bills, and got evicted. I now have a job and am earning good money but can't find a place that will accept me." Some problems are easy for prospects to share. Others are embarrassing and painful. Your ability to address the prospect's problems (including the potential ones) is what will separate you from your competition.

When a prospect believes that you are the solution to their problem, they convert from prospect to client.

What problems do you solve for your customers? Do your offerings align with the problems they have, real or perceived? Use these questions to improve your conversion rate.

ACRE: Client Conversion

LET'S SAY YOU ARE A multifamily operator. Prospects are coming in for tours only to walk out just as fast, and your occupancy rate shows it. In order to stop the hemorrhaging of prospects and better understand the psychology of buyers, you read Paco Underhill's book *Why We Buy*.[16] Though it is mostly about retail, you customize it to your needs.

1. *Articulate the objective*: Your objective is simple: to increase the occupancy rate of the complex. To do this, you walk through the complex, attempting to see it from the perspective of the potential renter. Then you address signage issues that influence their first impression and improve the sensory aspects of the property by changing the lighting in the model units and adding background music in the common area. You also optimize the apartment layout; instead of showing a vacant unit, you stage it.

2. *Collect the metric*: You realize that while you could track the occupancy rate, it won't provide you with details about this part of the process. As a result, you decide to track the application

conversion rate. This is the number of applications submitted divided by the number of people who tour the complex.

3. **Rhythm**: You want to make better decisions more quickly; therefore, you track this ratio weekly. Each Monday, you look at this number to see your improvement from week to week.

4. **Evolve**: Determined to keep this number growing, you call and follow up with the people who toured but decided not to apply. You ask them for their honest feedback and they share that they didn't enjoy the music playing in the common area and were concerned that it had a disco party feel. This feedback allows you to adjust the music and improve the experience.

5. **Result**: As a result of continuously learning from those who didn't apply (or buy), you have made regular improvements to your presentation of the property in person and on your website. Your application ratio has improved and so has your occupancy rate.

TEAM ACTION: DEAL FLOW

THE DEAL FLOW LEVEL IS the most foundational level in the IPP. Just as we humans struggle to survive without oxygen, food, shelter, and other basic necessities, any business must address the core needs in this chapter to survive.

The very first core need at this level is Lifestyle Congruence. Although that section in this chapter is geared toward the investor, it also applies to you. In my career, I've had many managers tell me that my compensation was directly tied to the value I created for the organization. One manager had me keep a log of the value I created, and we went over it during my annual performance reviews. He told me that he expected me to produce ten dollars' worth of value for each dollar I was paid. For example, if I earned $20,000, he wanted to see me generate a minimum of $200,000 in value. If I had been in accounting, he would have loved to see how I contributed to revenue increases or expense reductions. If you want to make more money, you need to produce more value for the company. Determining exactly how that value is produced should be a conversation between you and your manager.

Real estate is capital-intensive, and the company needs capital to do more deals. Not every real estate business needs a constant influx of capital; some only need it when they are ready for their next acquisition. You should understand the capital requirements of the business, so ask your manager how you can help in that area.

When it comes to deal attraction, you can help seek out new deals that align with the company's acquisition targets. Everyone on my team is encouraged to learn how to do this. Finding the right deals is hard, and the more people looking in the marketplace, the better.

Chapter 4

CREATE PERMANENT PROFIT

IN THE ORIGINAL *FIX THIS NEXT*, MIKE WROTE, "A REINVESTED 'profit' is an expense. Period."[17] Reading these words had a powerful impact on me because it's not the way we normally think about profit. I have an accounting degree, and from my first accounting class, I was taught that all profits are the profits of the business, including the reinvested portion.

When it comes time to pay your personal expenses and support your lifestyle, reinvested profits will not help you. You need the business to produce cash and distribute that cash to you.

My grandmother worked for a large grocery store chain. When I was a child, she had the opportunity to purchase stock in the company, and she bought some shares for me. Now, as a shareholder, I receive a dividend check every quarter. My last check represented $.43 for each share I own. However, according to its financial statements, the company earned $1.30 in profit per share. So where is the rest of the "profit"? Not paid to the shareholders, that's for sure. If I relied on the traditional definition of profit to pay my bills, I'd call up the corporate office and say, "Hey, where is the rest of my portion of the profits?"

Profit is what you take out of the business. Period.

Besides money to support our lives, profit has another important function. A steady flow of profit brings stability to us and our partners, investors, and team members.

We can't have a conversation about profit without mentioning two must-read books. The first is *Profit First* by Mike Michalowicz. In it, Mike shares how business owners should think about profit and expense management.[18] When leading workshops and in my live classes, I hear people mention his Profit First system all the time. If you want to know how I implement it, you can find a free training on www.FixThisNextForRealEstateInvestors.com.

The second book to consider is *Profit First for Real Estate Professionals* by David Richter. In his book, David modifies Mike's Profit First methodology specifically for real estate investors.[19]

As you work through this fundamental need, keep in mind our goal: to maximize the profits—our definition of the word—that you can generate from the business.

NEED #1: DEBT ERADICATION

Question: Do you consistently remove debt rather than accumulate it?

Acquiring debt is easy. And hopefully the social media algorithms don't get wind of the fact that you are a real estate investor, because if they do you, will be barraged by posts about good debt vs. bad debt. This debate is about as old as Mac vs. Windows or Chevy vs. Ford.

If Dave Ramsey were to enter the conversation, he would likely say, "The only good debt is no debt." His point is that when you hold debt, you introduce risk into the equation. Personal or business debt represents a financial risk. Business ownership is its own financial risk. Combining the two creates the potential for double trouble.

For our purposes, "bad debt" represents funds leaving your business without an offsetting income component, like a business credit card that carries a monthly balance and is used to cover working capital expenses; whereas "good debt" brings in more cash than the outflow used to service the debt.

It's not uncommon for real estate investors to use debt to finance properties. Debt not only makes it easier to acquire properties; it also creates leverage that increases cash-on-cash returns. We will talk about the use of leverage in the Profitability Leverage core need section.

While this core need's primary focus is on the eradication of bad debt, we can use it to reduce all liabilities. The more we lower our debt, the more we lower risks that have the potential to wipe us out.

Property loans wiped out Dave Ramsey. By the age of twenty-six, he owned four million dollars' worth of real estate; but then his primary bank called in loans with a balance of $1.2 million and, shortly thereafter, a second bank called in loans amounting to $800,000. He was able to repay all but around $400,000 of the loans before filing bankruptcy. This event changed the way he thought about debt, and he determined that all of his future real estate holdings would be paid for with cash.[20]

Each of us has a different level of risk tolerance, and whether our goal is to eliminate all the debt from our business or just the bad debt, we need a plan. The first step is to stop using debt to cover expenses. Next, we need to fix our cash flow situation. Every time we use debt to cover today's expenses, we borrow from our future cash flows. Most likely, the root cause of this problem is that we don't have enough cash flowing into the business today. Or maybe the income is good but our expenses are too high and we are bleeding cash.

Faced with this situation, we have two options: increase revenue or decrease costs.

You might feel like it will be difficult to cut expenses. You're right; cutting costs is challenging. Just remember that if you cut something and later determine that you need it, you can always restart the service.

Sometimes our vendors protect their revenue stream by making it hard for us to leave. When my business was new, I used the services of an outsourced provider to take care of some office tasks. For fifty dollars per month, I had access to fifteen tasks per month. Each task equaled up to twenty minutes of work. If I needed them to sit on hold for me for one hour, that was three tasks. If I didn't use all the tasks in a given month they rolled over, and they never expired. I never used all my credits, so every month, a few more tasks rolled over.

As my business grew, I expanded my team and rarely used this service, but I did continue paying for it. I didn't want to cancel because of the rolling credits. Every month, like clockwork, they collected their fifty dollars, and I gladly paid it because I had credits for future work in case I needed it. Every month my bookkeeper asked me if I was using the service, and every month I said no. Every month she asked me if I wanted to cancel it, and every month I said no.

Then she pulled out the big guns. "Scott, you are the embodiment of the sunk cost fallacy. How many credits are you trying to accumulate?"

She was right. I canceled the service that day with over 700 credits. I admit, it was painful to give up all those credits at the time, but I have not thought twice about the service for years. It was a waste of money to keep it going.

Cutting our expenses should reduce our need to use debt. Then we can apply a debt reduction strategy to start trimming our debt load.

One strategy for eliminating the debt is to follow the debt snowball method taught by Dave Ramsey:

1. Make a list of all your debt balances.
2. Identify the debt with the lowest balance.
3. Continue making all the current minimum payments.
4. When the lowest-balance debt is paid off, begin applying that minimum payment to the debt with the next lowest balance.
5. Continue until all the debt is eradicated.

With the bad debt gone, guess what? You now need to go back and recalculate your Lifestyle Congruence, which was discussed in Chapter 3, Need #1. Your new freedom number should be lower.

But what about good debt?

One of the arguments often made about using leverage to purchase property is that the tenants are the ones paying off the loans. While technically true, one of the challenges with commercial debt is that the loans are amortized for a longer period than their call date—meaning that the bank calculates the payments as if they are spread over twenty or twenty-five years, but the loans will have balloon payments due in three to five years.

Let's say we have a $800,000 loan, with a 6% interest rate, amortized over twenty years (240 payments) with a balloon payment due in five years. At the end of the fifth year, we must either repay the entire outstanding balance or refinance the property with a new loan.

There is further potential risk here. We assume that when it's time to refinance, the banks will be in the lending mood. But what if we get to that point and banks aren't lending? Think of any recessionary period. If refinancing is not possible, what is your plan?

This is why we want to remove as much debt as possible. Debt can affect a company's stability, so let's eradicate that risk.

ACRE: Debt Eradication

FOR THIS ACRE, WE'LL USE Mike's approach in *Fix This Next*, slightly modified for the ACRE framework.

Before we do, I should tell you that Mike didn't use the ACRE framework in *Fix This Next*. He should have, but he didn't. Instead, he used the OMEN (objective, measurement, evaluation, nurture) framework. I have modified this section from his book into the ACRE framework that we use.[21]

Let's pretend that flipping houses has been your dream ever since you saw your first episode of *Fixer Upper* with Joanna and Chip Gaines on HGTV. There are tons of deals to be had out there; you just need seed money. The thing is, you don't have any money left.

Your business is living off loans, and your FTN analysis identified that your vital need is to eradicate debt.

Here's how you work the ACRE plan:

1. ***Articulate the objective***: Debt isn't bad if it drives profit; debt is bad when you are beholden to it. You decide that over time, you will wipe out your loans and become your own bank. You will always have at least 20% of the average purchase price for a house in your area in the bank, in cash. You can move decisively with this and won't have to hook or crook your way through purchases. Currently, you have zero cash and $100,000 in debt.

To wipe out debt, you will use 5% of the top-line sale price of each of your home sales. You sell houses for $300,000 on average, which means that you will put $15,000 toward your debt each time. By your seventh flip, you plan to have eradicated the debt. For now, it is hand to mouth—or, as you like to say, flip to flop. But that is about to change.

2. **Collect the metric**: You set up an account using the Profit First methodology and label it "Flip Funds." The average house you buy is $200,000 and repairs are usually $40,000, so you commit to having $48,000 or more in that account within twelve months.

3. **Rhythm**: Money is not a constant stream for you. It comes (and goes) in tidal waves. When you sell a house, money flows in. When you buy and renovate a house, money flows out. So you decide to set up a debrief and evaluation after every real estate transaction, which is about once every two or three months.

4. **Evolve**: While you have contractors, you are in the business alone, so you don't have a team to give you hands-on guidance as you build your cache of cash. However, you do put one hundred rocks, each with "$1,000" painted on it, on your conference table. After each flip, you take away the quantity of rocks that represents the amount of debt you have paid down. Once all the rocks are gone, so is the burden of debt.

Great visual! To address the "become your own bank" part, you set up a big posterboard in your office with "20%" written on it, indicating the money you will immediately allocate from every sale to your Flip Funds account. After every transaction, you write the current balance in the Flip Funds account on your posterboard.

5. **Result**: Over the following year, you sell several properties and allocate more than $200,000 to the Flip Funds account. The next good deal that comes through is for a $175,000 house that you could likely sell for $250,000 within four weeks. You have the cash to put down 20%. Shoot, you could even put down 100% and still have $25,000 to do the repairs. More good deals will come, and you will be able to take advantage of them if they are a good fit for your company. The best part? No rocks in the conference room.

NEED #2: PROFITABLE LEVERAGE

Question: When debt is used, is it to generate predictable, increased profitability?

As investors, we know that debt plays a vital role in most real estate transactions. According to the Mortgage Bankers Association, in 2023, "Total commercial real estate (CRE) mortgage borrowing and lending is estimated to have totaled $429 billion" and lending was down by 47% from 2022 because of the rising interest rate environment.[22]

When used correctly, debt can help you generate predictable and increased profitability. Another benefit of using debt is that it allows for the purchase of multiple properties, which may help with a building a more diverse portfolio.

A frequent example I hear cited by multifamily investors is a comparison between a financed ten-unit complex compared to a single-family house that was paid for with cash. With the ten-unit complex, having one unit vacant leaves you with a 10% vacancy rate. However, if you own the one house and it's vacant, you have a 100%

vacancy rate. This example shows the power that the use of debt gives to the investor to help them mitigate risk.

While debt leverage can help investors maximize returns, it also exposes them to greater risk. In core need #1, Debt Eradication, we discussed one of the risks associated with refinancing a property in the future. Investors get crushed by debt when they fail to have a plan to mitigate the credit risk.

For example, Frank Rolfe, the fifth-largest mobile home park operator in the US we discussed in Chapter 3, has figured out that his ideal loan structure occurs when he can negotiate a maturity or balloon period of eight years with the bank. As he puts it, eight years is two presidential cycles. That gives you adequate time to start working on your refinancing plan while paying attention to the macroeconomic issues that could affect it. And hopefully, the net operating income of the asset has risen prior to that refinancing period, making the refinancing process a lot easier.

The goal is to only use good debt to generate predictable and profitable revenue, but also have a plan to mitigate the associated risk.

Notice the keywords in that last sentence. The criterion for good debt is that it creates predictable and profitable revenue.

Susan, one of my IPP beta testers, shared with me how she used this core need to help her navigate a decision at her park. She owns a mobile home park in North Carolina where the laundry room equipment was old and prone to disrepair. She was on the fence about purchasing new equipment; while she knew it needed to be done, she debated whether to pay cash or use financing. She didn't want to pay cash and have money sitting idle in equipment, but she didn't want to incur more debt either. In her mind, this would be bad debt. After working through this part of the IPP, she generated a *pro forma* statement based on new equipment that worked consistently. She could see that the return on investment would be positive and met the requirements of this core need. Financing the equipment would increase revenue. Additionally, the extra profitable revenue would have a positive return upon the sale of the park, which she was considering.

But what if the revenue wasn't profitable?

Scan almost any real estate forum and you are sure to find someone asking about a property that currently produces negative cash flow or at best breaks even. Such posts almost always contain a statement that in the future, when they can raise rents, it will be profitable. After a long, painful read, there it is, the obvious question: "Should I do it?"

Then come the predictable comments: "It's not a good deal" or "I only buy properties that produce cash flow from day one." In some cases, the internet trolls come out and totally destroy the poster. It's easy to get deal anxiety and want to acquire a property so badly that you try and force the projections to work, even though in your heart you know they won't. If you find yourself in this mindset, stop. You have the number one telltale sign of got-to-do-a-deal-itis.

Real estate developer Richard Michael Abraham taught me that in this situation, "You are likely to wind up where you start." Meaning that if you take shortcuts in your *pro forma* statement or try to force the numbers to work, you will end up with a project that is a disaster both financially and for your reputation.

Using debt for investments that do not generate positive cash flow from the start is not good debt, and our goal is to use debt only when it will create profitable leverage for our operation.

ACRE: Profitable Leverage

IN THIS ACRE EXAMPLE, LET'S consider a multifamily operator who needs to determine if a value-add project should be financed.

1. ***Articulate the objective***: The objective is to use debt financing to enhance the profitability of a property, putting the funds toward improving the amenities center in one of the complexes owned by the operator. While the amenities center currently works, the operator believes that updating it will increase revenues.

2. ***Collect the metric***: The investors expect a 20% cash-on-cash return and, according to the *pro forma* statement, the new revenue will generate the desired return if leverage is used. If debt is not used, the incremental revenue will only produce a 12% return. To evaluate performance, the operator will track:
   - ***Incremental revenue***: Is the center producing the desired revenue?
   - ***Return on investment***: The target is 20%.

3. ***Rhythm***: Each month, the operator will compare the expected revenue with the actual revenue to determine whether the center is producing the desired result. They will also track improvement in return on investment to make sure they are hitting the numbers.

4. ***Evolve***: A thorough analysis was conducted. Prospective residents were asked what value the improved center would bring to them, and that feedback was incorporated into the marketing for the complex. Also, the center is now spotlit on all property tours. To achieve the target, project costs are tightly controlled.

A plan has been established to reduce operating expenses in the complex to offset any deficiencies in case the new revenue target is not achieved. This alternate plan will ensure that the use of the debt produces the desired return on investment for the partners.

5. **Result**: After the first year, the amenity center fell short of increasing the revenue number. It was determined that the forecast was too optimistic, which resulted in the missed target. This required the operator to execute on plan B and cut other costs at the complex to achieve the target return on investment.

NEED #3: MARGIN HEALTH

Question: Do you have healthy profits within each of your offerings, and do you continually seek ways to increase them?

The wording of this question is important. Our goal is to have *healthy* profits, and we need to work steadily on increasing them. Remember, you have two options to up your company's profit: raise prices or cut expenses. The next time you hear yourself or other investors talk about thinning margins, you'll know the solutions to that problem.

Cutting costs is easy. First, sit down and review all the cash outflows of the company. Cancel unnecessary services or call the providers and ask for a discount. If they can't go lower, find other providers that will. In my experience, you can find expense-cutting opportunities within every company, though you can only cut so much.

Another consideration: Can any of the business expenses be transferred to the customer?

Take a mobile home park or multifamily unit that was originally built with a master meter. A master meter situation occurs when the power or water company only installed one meter for their utility. The utility company bills the complex for all the usage, and the complex then pays for all the usage, including the waste. None of that cost is shouldered by the tenants.

I own several condo rental units and none of them have their own water bill; it's paid for as part of the monthly assessment. Guess what: There are no consequences for the parties who allow their toilets to leak or leave the water running all day long. The condo associations perform annual toilet testing to look for water leaks, so that's one strategy to cut costs if the conversion from master meter is cost-prohibitive.

If we still want to increase profits after cutting expenses, we need to raise our prices—and that's sometimes hard.

Let me tell you about my friend Mike Cinnante. First and foremost, he's a super nice guy. I'll use my author superpowers and declare him the greatest car detailer in the Tampa area. Mike's eye for detail is second to none, which is why I think he's the best. He offers a mobile detailing service, and not only does he provide annual detailing, he also provides biweekly or monthly services. Recently, as he wrapped up my monthly service, he hesitated and then said, "Hey, next month I have to raise my prices slightly."

I could tell he felt bad. I asked, "When was the last time you raised your prices?"

"It's been close to five years."

"Five years? Why are you not raising them annually?"

Mike said, "I know that costs for everything are going up, and I don't want my services to be a burden for my customers."

In the five years that Mike did not raise his prices, his own expenses increased, resulting in him shouldering the burden for his customers. That's not fair to Mike.

I also see this pattern with lawn service providers, pool cleaners, and so many other service providers. They get their prices locked in one time and then hesitate to raise their prices. They are afraid of losing customers.

Do you know who else does this? Real estate investors. Many operators avoid increasing rents, fees, prices, etc. because they are afraid that they will lose customers. Therefore, they shoulder decreasing margins while their customers continue to get a great deal.

This is very common. Just look through the listings on any commercial listing service. I reviewed one of these services and counted over 4,000 listings containing the phrase "below-market rent."

When I ask investors why they don't raise their rents annually, the answer is always the same; they don't want to upset the residents. But after years of failing to keep up with market rents, residents will one day face a large rent increase that is more upsetting to them than predictable yearly changes. In one online community forum I visited, a resident was upset because her new landlord adjusted her rent to the market price. In the comments, someone posted: "I'm going to hug my landlord next month. She's not raised my rent in seven years." How does that help the resident or the landlord?

Given increasing costs, failure to keep up with market rates makes it harder to maintain the property. This means that residents who love their homes will ultimately and increasingly see deferred maintenance. This leads to a lower valuation on sale, and one of the first plays most new owners make is to raise the rent to the market rate.

That increase will result in a shock to tenants' wallets and be harder for their budgets to absorb. They would be better off with predictable annual adjustments.

ACRE: Margin Health

IT'S TIME FOR ANOTHER ACRE. This time, we'll look at how we can use automation to reduce the expenses associated with showing our properties.

1. *Articulate the objective*: You want to implement technology to streamline your operation and make it less human-dependent. To do this, you plan to use a self-guided touring system that allows potential renters to view the property without having to interface with a human. However, you are concerned that the lack of human interaction might increase the time it takes to rent the unit.

2. *Collect the metric*: To ensure that your occupancy rate is not affected, you decide to track the following metrics:
   - *Viewings to application*: Currently, 9% of viewers generate an application. Realizing that without a human involved, this number is likely to decrease, your target for success is 5% or higher.
   - *Average days to rent*: It typically takes your team twenty-seven days to rent an open unit. The savings you generate from not having an employee showing the unit will allow you to let the unit sit open longer. You will reduce your cost if the average days to rent is less than fifty-four.

3. **Rhythm**: You decide to review the metrics monthly. Because this is a test program, multiple updates are important. You also determine to run the program for six months.

4. **Evolve**: As prospective tenants come to the property to tour available units, you capture their email addresses and phone numbers. Using this information, you can retarget them with follow-up messages. The old method meant that property managers had to add email addresses to the CRM manually; now, the email capture is automated and 100% of the viewers are added to the email list.

5. **Result**: After the six-month test pilot, the results were mixed. The viewing per application rate was weaker than expected, resulting in only four applications per one hundred viewers. However, the average number of days to rent increased only slightly, to thirty-two. As a result, you realize that converting to the self-guided program will reduce costs and decide to implement it further.

NEED #4: TRANSACTION FREQUENCY

Question: Do you maximize your revenue from each client?

Welcome to what I think is one of the most difficult core needs for many businesses. In fact, I believe that real estate investors—and probably one other type of business owner—have it the hardest. The good news is that the other group might have figured this out, and now it's our turn. I will share the identity of this other group shortly.

The goal of this core need is to maximize the revenue generated from our clients. Think of McDonald's asking if you want fries with your order. Another example is the rental car companies who sell protection for the vehicles, offer refueling services, and rent car seats.

The challenge for us is that we don't have much to upsell. Think of house flippers. They get a property under contract, renovate it, and then list it on the market. The buyer pays the market price for the home and, well, that's it. Transaction over. This is what makes this core need so difficult. But when you do find ways to generate more revenue from each client, your business will instantly become more profitable.

At the beginning of this chapter, I mentioned another group who struggle with this core need. In *Fix This Next*, the original version of this core need question reads: "Do your clients repeatedly buy from you over alternatives?"[23]

Imagine Mike Michalowicz then presenting onstage to the NFDA—the National Funeral Directors Association—and trying to explain how they could meet this core need. It's an almost impossible challenge, right? How many times can they call their customers and ask them to buy more services? I mean, they could call, but the customers probably won't answer.

Funeral directors and real estate investors have this in common. Being able to sell to the same customer is challenging, and we have to hunt for the opportunities.

In my niche of land investing, it's common to sell multiple properties to the same customer. In self-storage, same thing, a customer can have multiple units with you or heck, your competition. Wholesalers, yeah, you get repeat customers as well. Selling to your existing customer base will bring you many benefits. First, it's much easier. Your customer already knows you and more importantly, they trust you. They know what the customer experience will be like. Second, not having to market to find new customers means your customer acquisition cost is lower. If you can sell multiple times to your existing customer, do you have a system in place to contact them with new offers?

It's super easy to put them on your email distribution list and send them emails with specials or featured properties, but the gold is getting them on the phone. Picking up the phone might be scary, but if you want to generate more sales from your existing customers, that's the secret.

Investors in all real estate niches, including house flippers and multifamily-unit investors, can address the core need question: Do you maximize your revenue from each client?

Satisfying this need will require some creative thinking and different approaches. It will also require testing different concepts to find the ones that work.

For the funeral directors, the answer did not come from transaction frequency, but from offering other services. In *Fix This Next*, Mike outlines three ways to increase transaction frequency.

"The first is to have the same customer buy repeatedly—which may work for you, but these funeral folks? Not so much. The second is to offer complementary services and/or products without diluting your offering. And the third is to do both. For the funeral directors, we went with option two. Coffins, flowers, enhanced services are all options. Going further, one funeral home teamed up with a portrait painter to do painted memorials (and took a little piece of the action)."[24]

Self-storage operators have mastered this second option of providing complementary services. They sell protection, locks, packing supplies, some provide U-Haul services, and that is only the start of the list. These operators continuously look for ways to generate more revenue from their same customer base. These ancillary services generate an additional 7-10% in revenue.

What services can you provide that will complement your customers' needs? To get creative, I think it's important to think about where you are in the buying process. Thinking about the customer journey and where you fit into it will give you some insight into what came before you and what will come after.

If you don't know where you fit, ask them. Here are two powerful questions I like to ask: "What did you do before buying this property?" and "What services did you use to get here?" In the self-storage world, it is easy to see that the customers show up in rental trucks to move stuff in. True, not all of them do, but enough for those operators to understand where they sit in the customer journey: Their customers need transportation first.

What comes after you, for your client? Try asking them this question: "Now that you have closed on [insert your words here], what comes next for you?"

Being curious about your customers can have a huge impact. One thing we noticed in my business is that after closing, the next step is a survey. Because we do owner financing on the majority of our properties, it is easy for us to offer to have the property surveyed and add the cost of that survey into the financed amount at a markup. This not only gives us incremental revenue from each transaction, it also helps our customer. It's a true win-win.

Brainstorm with your team about services you can add. How do you fit into your customer's story? Can you remove friction for them so that they want to do business with you again? Can you offer more services? These are just a few of the questions you can use as prompts to get the ideas flowing.

ACRE: Transaction Frequency

IN THIS ACRE, WE WILL create a way to increase your revenues.

1. ***Articulate the objective***: You own several rental properties and want to increase the average unit income while staying competitive with market rates, so you gather the team around the whiteboard for a good old brainstorming session. "What service can we provide to our clients to generate more income?" One idea is to provide unemployment rent protection. If a tenant participates in the program and loses their job, the protection will cover their rent payments for three months as they find new employment. The average rent is $1,800 per month. Based on calculating the risk, you determine that if you hit the metrics, the protection option will cost each participating resident $50 per month. (The math supporting this ACRE can be found in the resources at www.FixThisNextForRealEstateInvestors.com.)

2. ***Collect the metric***: To track the success of this program, you decide to monitor the following metrics:
   - ***Participation rate***: The percentage of tenants joining the protection program. The goal is for 25% of tenants to enroll.
   - ***Usage rate***: You calculate that to remain profitable, the number of participating tenants actually using the coverage must be 10% or less. Measuring the usage rate will allow you to determine if the monthly rate needs to be adjusted.

3. ***Rhythm***: Because of the importance of these metrics, you track them on a monthly basis. Each month when you review the results, you consider whether an adjustment to the monthly rate is needed.

4. **Evolve**: To ensure that you have the money set aside to cover program usage, you follow the Profit First strategy of opening a dedicated bank account. You call this the "Unemployment Fund." Each month when you collect the protection revenue from the tenants, you deposit the funds into this account. Should a tenant need the use the protection, you withdraw their rent from this account and move it to your general account.

5. **Result**: By the end of the first year, you achieve a participation rate of 30%; your tenants love the idea, and knowing that you are looking out for them. The unemployment rate in your area averages 4%, but your tenants have a higher-than-average unemployment rate. You determine that 8% of the participants use the protection. To your surprise, your tenants don't need three full months of coverage because the average period of unemployment is 2.25 months, so the benefit costs you less than expected. Of your eighty tenants, twenty-four participate, generating $14,400 in revenue. Of these participants, you have two claims totaling $8,100. This leaves you with a profit of $6,300 while fulfilling your goal of generating more revenue.

NEED #5: CASH RESERVES

Question: Does the business have enough cash reserves to cover all expenses for three months or longer?

I hate when I have cash sitting idle. I feel guilty. But I'm here to say that you do not need to feel guilty about sitting on as much cash as you want. You have permission. I can't tell you how many times someone has told me that they are surprised by the amount of cash I prefer to keep available. I get it, inflation is eroding it, blah, blah, blah.

At the end of 2024, Warren Buffet's company, Berkshire Hathaway, had over $275 billion in cash. This money is not invested in the market: It's just sitting there. OK, OK, maybe it's not just sitting in a bank; I'm sure it's invested in treasury bills for some short-term interest. But the point is that it's probably underperforming compared to what it could be doing if it were invested in the market.

If idle cash is bad, how much cash should you hold? The correct answer is that it depends on you. Ask one hundred people and you would probably get ninety answers. Although I don't know the exact amount that you should keep on hand, I do know that there is a minimum amount you need to sock away for those rainy days. My answer is cash reserves that will cover a minimum of three months' worth of expenses. And guess what, if it helps you sleep better knowing you have six months' worth, then that's your answer.

One of the first things pilots learn is that they should establish their own personal minimums. These are the minimum-quality operating conditions that a pilot will fly in. The Federal Aviation Administration (FAA) has minimum flying conditions for all types of flights. For example, some flights might require three miles of visibility, but a pilot might choose to not fly if the visibility is less than five miles. Just because a flight could take place doesn't mean the pilot is capable of handling it. To ensure that pilots don't fly beyond their personal capabilities, the FAA encourages all pilots to set their own personal minimums.

What is your personal minimum in cash reserves that you wish to keep available?

The reality facing all of us is that we just don't know what's coming. As much as we might think we have the future dialed in, history shows that we don't. As Stanford professor Scott Sagan says, "Things that never happened before happen all the time."[25]

Black swan events happen all the time. Who would have envisioned a global pandemic—and the response—where the entire world practically shut down? During this difficult time, many landlords lost the ability to collect rent from tenants because the government implemented rent and eviction freezes, yet they still had to pay their mortgages.

The best way to foster stability is to be prepared for these "never before" events.

ACRE: Cash Reserves

YOU KNOW YOU NEED TO have a three-month cash reserve, but you are a little short. About three months short. But that's OK because you can always start today. It's ACRE time.

1. *Articulate the objective*: Your goal is to build a cash reserve that could cover your operating costs for three months. You determine that you need $20,000 a month to cover these expenses. That means you need a minimum of $60,000 in the bank. You open a bank account and call it the "Vault."
2. *Collect the metrics*: The metric is simple: cash in this special account. You want to have $60,000 in your Vault account within twelve months.
3. *Rhythm*: To ensure that the account keeps growing, and to make it happen on autopilot, you allocate 3% of your revenue

to the Vault. You check the balance on the fifteenth and the last day of each month.

4. *Evolve*: Throughout this chapter, you have identified ways to reduce expenses, increase profit margins, and add revenue. Now is the time to reap those newfound profits. Capture them in the Vault until you reach your goal.

5. *Result*: You might run into challenges on the journey to building this account. Maybe you can't contribute for months. It's OK. Goals are great, but if it takes you two years instead of one, who cares? You did it. Also, look for ways to make it fun. Create posters with slogans like "Three for Three" (3% for three months' worth of reserves) or "From Small Savings to a Secured Future." Don't stop until you *are* secured.

TEAM ACTION: CREATE PERMANENT PROFIT

YOUR MANAGER NEEDS YOU TO help them be accountable. Profitability is everyone's responsibility, and the profitability of the organization supports your stability. The way you bring ideas to leadership is dependent on their approachability, but here are some ways you can add to the profitability.

- Share any ideas you have that will save money. At my company, we had an employee who saw that our phone was costing us $130 per month. They pointed out that since we use Microsoft Teams, we could switch and save $720 per year (net of teams). While this savings is not massive, it sure does help to build up the cash reserves.

- Think outside the box. At one point in my career, I was responsible for overseeing a company-wide spending freeze. Some of the team members began asking me for permission to order office supplies. Trying to be creative, I grabbed an empty copy paper box and went from desk to desk, asking for extra pens, Post-it notes and other supplies my colleagues could part with. In one office alone, I collected three boxes full of supplies. The supply hoarders were not happy with me.

- Do you have ideas for revenue opportunities? What do your customers ask you for that you don't offer? Share your ideas with leadership.

- If you have a good relationship with your manager, it's OK to harass them monthly, like the story I tell in the Debt Eradication core need section about letting my subscription keep renewing even though I wasn't using the service. If your manager doesn't like being reminded every month, it's OK to tell them that I sent you. I've got your back!

- Remember that sometimes, the investor or leadership is busy or engaged with a different or bigger issue and may not be ready to hear about your idea. Don't take it personally; add it to a list and float the idea again later.

Chapter 5

ACHIEVE ORGANIZATIONAL ORDER

PASSIVE INCOME IS A MYTH. IT DOESN'T EXIST.

As I write these words, I can hear the gasps of all those who hold it up as the reason to invest in real estate. Now, before you throw the book across the room and come looking for me, hear me out.

True passive income does not exist. The closest thing I have been able to find is the inheritance of a dividend-paying stock. You didn't have to work for the original capital and all you have to do is monitor the dividend deposits, reinvesting or spending the money. Either way, this still requires work. The same is true for real estate. Although passive streams of income may be coming in, some work is still required to support them. Therefore, these income streams should be thought of as *less active* rather than passive.

I admit, in the past, I have been known to use the phrase "passive income." But as of today, I will not, for one simple reason: I believe it gives us a false perception of reality, a mental picture of money streaming into our bank accounts while we sit on the beach, enjoying our best lives. We all want money to flow to us nonstop and without personal effort, but all income streams require effort.

The reality is, we should be working to create companies that produce recurring positive cash flows. This better describes our target and puts us in the right mindset. The figure below shows our ideal situation, which is to generate as much positive cash flow as we can using the lowest level of personal effort required.

RECURRING POSITIVE CASH FLOW

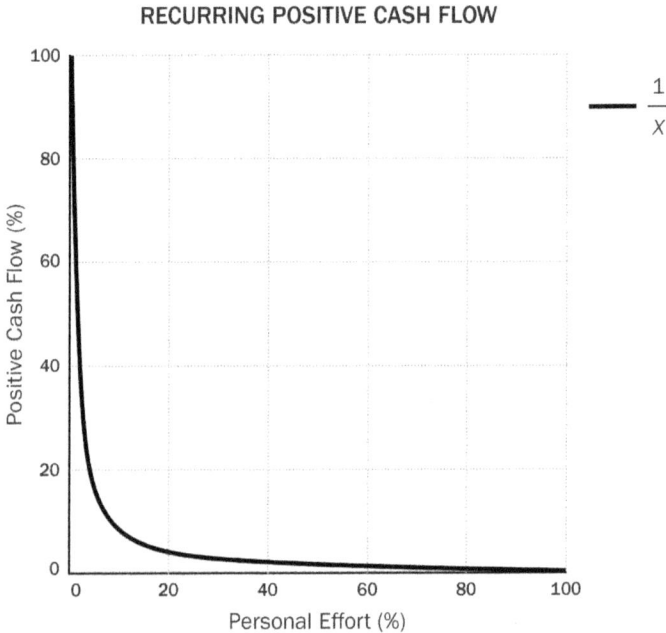

Figure 8: Recurring Positive Cash Flow

That last sentence is important. Let's break it down, starting with "ideal situation." This means we can come close but will likely never reach it.

Calculus was one of the college classes I struggled with most. I just did not connect with the whole concept of limits and derivatives. But today, I have a better understanding of limits. Although our goal might be to have 100% of our income require no personal effort, that is impossible. It's like trying to touch the end of the rainbow; we can see it, but we can't physically get there.

The next important phrase in that sentence is "positive cash flow." As I discussed in the Profitable Leverage section in Chapter 4, doing something today that does not produce positive cash flow today will not move us closer to our goal. Cash flow must be positive from the start. I've seen so many instances where investors have a lease option on a property and their outgoing payment is greater than the amount they receive from their buyer. They are hoping for price appreciation, but this is speculation, not investing.

As we continue to analyze the sentence, pay special attention to the phrase "lowest level of personal effort required." This isn't about our effort—it's where our team steps in. In the corporate world, leaders set the vision and managers and employees make it a reality. You won't find the CEO of Amazon coding the website, working in the warehouse, or delivering the packages. No, they leave all that work to the employees so that they can concentrate on how the company will operate in the future. In 2018, Jeff Bezos told *Forbes*, "Friends congratulate me after a quarterly-earnings announcement and say, 'Good job, great quarter,' and I'll say, 'Thank you, but that quarter was baked three years ago.'"[26]

Your goal is to generate 100% of your income from recurring positive cash flows while expending as little personal effort as possible. Achieving this will allow you to enjoy the time freedom you want while also giving you time to focus on strategy.

Cash flows do not live on forever. All assets have a maximum production lifetime. For example, a rental house generates cash flow as long as you own and rent it. In land investing, the cash flow stream stops when the loan is paid in full, which could happen in one day or twenty years.

This chapter is about the Order level of the IPP. Here, we shift from the work being dependent on us to the empowerment of our teams. This level is about building efficiencies to make our organizations strong and operate like clockwork.

Funnily enough, this is also the level I see most real estate investors working in when they should be working on the Deal Flow or Profit levels. Addressing this level too soon brings risk to your business.

Billy, an attendee in one of the workshops I led, explained how much work he had done to create his processes and scripts. When I asked Billy how many sales he had, he said zero. He was putting his time into building systems and scripts for his future team because he wanted them to know what to do. The issue here is obvious; you see it. Building systems and processes while not actually doing the work in real time is a waste because you are working on hypothetical situations.

Most entrepreneurs overthink the onboarding of new employees. We hear about the value of playbooks, processes, and systems and believe we have to create them to show new employees exactly how to do the work. The problem is that we marginalize our employees so that they end up completing mindless tasks just to follow a playbook. No one wants to work in a job where they are not free to use their mind, free to find solutions. Instead of giving them a playbook, let's show them how we do the work and then ask them to document their process. You want teams where each contributor uses their brainpower to get the task done in the most efficient way. When team members can identify problems and navigate them without involving you or their managers, you achieve major momentum toward your goals.

Mike Michalowicz uses a great analogy, explaining that when business owners jump into processes to help, they act like superheroes coming to the rescue. Think about the plot of any *Batman* movie. The chief of police loses control of Gotham; he can't do his job. He runs out to the Bat-Signal and fires it up to summon Batman. Seeing the signal, our superhero gets into the Batmobile and races into town. He finds the bad guys and a fight ensues. BAM! BONK! POW! After an intense battle, our hero destroys the enemy, but in the process, he does something else. As the camera fades out, all you see is smoke, fire, and what remains of the destroyed city, but who cares, right? Just as in *Batman* movies, the team needs help and the manager swoops in, leaving a trail of destruction in their wake. As leaders, it's up to us to change the way we answer the call for help.

Order is about empowering your team and building a company that is less dependent on you or other key people. Let's now work to make you irrelevant to your business's success.

CORE NEED #1: MINIMIZED WASTED EFFORT

Question: Do you have an ongoing, working model that helps you reduce bottlenecks, slowdowns, and inefficiencies?

Frank Hernandez operates a house-flipping business. When Frank took the IPP assessment, Minimized Wasted Effort came up as his vital need. Frank knew he had an issue with his acquisition process, but because he was busy with other things, he didn't address it. "Admittedly, I hoped the team would just figure it out," he told me. They didn't; they walked past the problem every day without ever thinking it should be fixed.

After taking the IPP assessment, he knew it was his time to dive into the swamp and face the monster. To get there, Frank assembled his acquisitions team and a pack of Post-it notes, and they began mapping out the entire acquisition workflow. When the team told him the first step, he wrote it on a Post-it, placed it on the wall, and asked, "Now what?" They shouted out the next step and he again jotted it down and added it on the wall. At the end, they could see how work flowed through the department.

Frank then asked them to go back and count the number of tasks currently involved in each step. His logic was that when the number of tasks was higher for one step, it would indicate a bottleneck in the process. As the team returned with the counts, he noticed higher counts at three steps:

1. The initial property evaluation,
2. The step where he approves the next step,
3. And the step where a property needs a second round of due diligence.

"Seeing where the work was stuck was such a powerful moment. I knew right where to start. I could also see that I was part of the problem." Like Batman swooping in, ultimately, Frank was the problem. But the root cause goes deeper. It's a systemic entrepreneurial issue that stems from how we perceive leadership.

Early in our careers as employees, we wish our bosses were in the trenches helping us instead of managing from the ivory tower. As we grow into leaders, we remember those feelings and when our team asks for help, we want to support them. We gladly jump in to fix something, get a dopamine hit, and believe that we have done what good leaders do: support the team. The opposite is true. Without knowing it, we have alienated the team and robbed them of the opportunity to learn how to solve the issue on their own. We have created a culture where employees are unable to think for themselves.

You know the saying "use it or lose it"? If we don't create an environment where our teams feel empowered to think for themselves, they lose their ability and confidence to deal with challenges on their own. Which is not our goal. We want them to fix the problems they encounter.

Frank told me, "Watching the team struggle was like being forced to watch someone run their fingernails across a chalkboard. I was tempted to start throwing out solutions, but I heard your voice telling me to stand down." Now is the time to sit back and let the team stumble through the problem. When the entire team walks through these issues together, they learn how to identify solutions and fix problems. Improved workflow becomes their solution and by default, their process. They own it now and can fix it when it breaks.

Frank's team spent about twenty-four hours over a one-week period refining their acquisition process. At the end, they had a new process designed to streamline the work.

First, they addressed approvals. They created a matrix that categorized deals as either green, yellow, or red. Green deals automatically move on to the next stage. Yellow deals require a review by Frank or his delegate before a decision is made. Red deals are rejected. Frank no longer needs to be involved in each deal. The bottleneck has been eliminated.

For the initial property evaluation bottleneck, the team created a rapid evaluation system, a matrix that allows the intake team to score properties during the initial property assessment. If a property passes, they proceed to the next step. This solution decreased the time a property spent at the initial evaluation phase by 40% and resulted in Frank's team evaluating 30% more properties than they did before implementing the matrix.

The final issue was the time spent on second visits to properties to gather data that wasn't captured the first time. The team determined that if they used video to capture the first visit, this would reduce the number of second visits. As a test, Frank invested in a 360° camera. Initial site visits are now recorded that way so the team can go back and watch parts of the video instead of making a second visit. Second visits are rarely needed now.

The beauty of Frank's experience is not just the improvements in the system, because there are always things that need to be fixed; it's that he learned how to empower the team to do it. He introduced them to *kaizen*, the Japanese concept of constant improvement, and they learned how to identify and solve issues that affect their work. Now they know how to fix problems before Frank needs to intervene.

This core need is not about fixing everything. This core need is fulfilled when there is an ongoing, working model to continually fix broken processes. The goal is to eliminate the mindset of working around broken processes or waiting for us to say, "Hey, this is broken." We want to create a culture where all team members are empowered to fix this next.

ACRE: Minimized Wasted Effort

YOU ARE A LAND-FLIPPING COMPANY, and it's time to get that due diligence process dialed in. You schedule a team meeting and get to work using ACRE to minimize wasted effort by creating a timeline map of the due diligence process.

1. ***Articulate the objective***: Your bottleneck is due diligence. You try adding people, but like a newly expanded highway, it runs smoothly for a few months and then the bottlenecks return. The objective is to streamline the process and reduce the amount of time it takes for a transaction to move through the due diligence process.

2. ***Collect the metrics***: The team meets and determines that they will regularly monitor two metrics:
   - ***Average time in due diligence***: The goal is to reduce the time spent on this process by 30%.
   - ***The number of steps in the due diligence process***: The goal is to eliminate five steps.

3. ***Rhythm***: You commit to reviewing the metrics every quarter. If the metrics are not showing progress, you will reassess the process and adjust as needed.

4. ***Evolve***: To kick off the initiative, the team lists each step in the due diligence process and estimates the time for each item. This gives them an estimate of the maximum time it takes to complete due diligence. As they work through these items, they look for ways to reduce the processing time. At the quarterly meeting, they provide you with updates on methods they have created to reduce the time it takes to complete tasks. Training is held monthly, by and for team members, where they share best practices with their peers so they can all benefit from the streamlined process.

5. **Result**: After the first three months, the team gathers with the manager to review their performance. To their surprise, they have reduced the average time a property spends in the due diligence process by 32%. This improvement means that the team can process more properties, saying goodbye to being the weakest link. The company benefits because its close ratio (purchase properties to mailings) increases, meaning that it is now more profitable.

CORE NEED #2: ROLE ALIGNMENT

Question: Are people's roles and responsibilities matched to their talents?

This will not come as a surprise, but research shows that employees perform better when they enjoy their work.[27] Shocking, right? Enjoying your job isn't just about having a nice manager, good pay, and fun work parties. Those things are great, but what employees want most is work that excites and energizes them.

We all have tasks that we love and some we loathe; it's true for me, you, and your employees. As leaders, we need to think differently about work, and that starts with role alignment. Meeting this core need gets everyone working in roles that play to their strengths.

Most jobs are built by categorizing tasks and compiling them in separate job descriptions. When you hire a bookkeeper, everything that is related to accounting, no matter how specialized, is assigned to them. If it smells like accounting, you give it to them even if they have no experience in that type of work. In one of my early roles, I was hired as the operations manager of a company. When the owners found out that I had an accounting degree, they asked me to "watch over" the accounting team. Those were two different jobs, and despite my degree, I had no experience leading an accounting staff.

But what if work was completed by the person on the team whose Zone of Excellence encompassed that work?

My executive assistant Alaine is fantastic. She has been an incredible addition to my team. The job description of an executive assistant is straightforward. Keep as much as possible off my plate, routing work where it needs to go. One Friday, during a one-on-one meeting, I mentioned that I needed one of our websites updated. She lit up; I could see the excitement in her eyes. A slight smile emerged as she said, "I can do it."

Surprised, I asked, "Have you updated websites in the past?"

"Yes, I enjoy it."

I asked Alaine to show me one, she shared her screen, and there it was, her work. Little did I know that my assistant was also good at creating websites. I described the project to her, told her what I wanted, provided her with some examples, and she was off. I knew that she was working in her Zone of Excellence when she asked for the brand kit. I explained that there wasn't one. She then asked about color scheme and where to find images and content.

All of this occurred on a Friday afternoon before a three-day holiday weekend.

When I returned on Tuesday, Alaine proudly presented the redesigned website that she had finished over the weekend. The site was great, but she had also created a brand kit for future use. This is the result of someone working in their Zone of Excellence.

Now imagine if you and your entire team worked exclusively in your Zones. What if we redesigned workflows not by department, but by individual Zones of Excellence?

That's what Frank Hernandez did for his business. Megan works as a project manager, overseeing contractors and keeping everything moving on renovations. She's also great at interviewing new team members. Yep, an HR job function is now handled by a project manager. Instead of assigning tasks to people in certain departments, a better way forward would be to assign work by a person's Zone of Excellence.

You might be thinking, *Yeah, that sounds great, but how do I know what a person's Zone of Excellence is?*

This will be a two-part process. In the first part, we will use a tool called Love–OK–Loathe (LOL). You can find a sample form below. Using this tool, we will ask the team to record the activities they perform in their jobs. Big, small, we want them all.

To the right of the activity are three columns: "Love," "OK," and "Loathe." These columns allow the team to reflect on work that is or is not in their Zones of Excellence by rating each activity.

ACTIVITY **JOURNAL** for the week of: ....

Activity	Love	OK	Loathe

Figure 9: Love–OK–Loathe (LOL)

Let's address a critical doubt right now. When you ask your team to list their tasks and then declare what they loathe about their jobs, it might freak them out. They may question what you plan to do with this information. They might not give you an honest answer. They might have nothing in the loathe column. This is because they are scared that if they tell you they don't like something, you will let them go. So, this is where you must be transparent. Start by explaining the Zone of Excellence—or have them read this book beforehand so they are working on the business with you.

Everyone needs to feel comfortable telling the truth about the work they are doing. Don't ask them to turn in the LOL—this list is for their eyes only—unless they want to share. The list will be used in part two of the process, a game we will play in the ACRE below.

This need is fulfilled when you have a process for ensuring that each member of the team is working in their Zone of Excellence.

ACRE: Role Alignment

LET'S PLAY A FUN GAME called Task Bingo. This is your team's chance to change things up.

1. *Articulate the objective*: We want our team to work in their Zones of Excellence. We gather them around the conference table and give everyone one index card. Each person chooses the task they are ready to dump and writes it on their card, and you use a collaboration tool so that remote team members can post their chosen tasks. You reassure the team, "It's okay that you loathe this task. Be honest and let's build work you love."

Your team will want anonymity; however, there's no hiding because everyone knows who currently does each task. With all the most loathed tasks on the table or board, it's time for the first ever Great Job Swap. Team members are encouraged to look over all the tasks displayed. If one looks interesting to them, they can pick up the card. Taking the card means they will learn more about the task from the person who currently does it. The goal is for the work to be reassigned to the people who are interested in it. At the end of the game, the remaining tasks are still owned by the current doers, but you now have the foundation for the job description of your next new hire. Yep, the new hire gets all the loathed tasks.

2. **Collect the metrics**: The first goal is to get each team member to have 80% of their tasks in the OK or Love columns. As the workload allocation improves, the goal is to have 80% of the tasks in the Love column, 20% in the OK, and 0% in the Loathe column.

3. **Rhythm**: With the goals identified, you play Task Bingo every quarter, or before a new employee joins the team.

4. **Evolve**: Workflows continue to evolve as new team members take on new assignments in their Zones of Excellence.

5. **Result**: With everyone working on tasks in their Zones of Excellence, production is through the roof. Deal flow is pumping, properties are moving, and mistakes are way down.

CORE NEED #3: OUTCOME DELEGATION

Question: Are the people closest to the problem empowered to resolve it?

Jamie, one of the managers on my team, is empowered to do the right thing for our customers. It's the culture of our business. One Tuesday afternoon she received a phone call. "Jamie, this is Jeremy," our client said. "I have a problem. I went to look at the land I just purchased and there are hundreds of tires out there. I don't know what I'm supposed to do. I guess I should have looked at the property before buying it." In my niche of owner-financed land, most people buy without looking at it first.

Jamie informed Jeremy that she would take care of it. After they hung up, she called Corey, one of our vendors, and explained the situation to him. A few days later, Corey went to the property and determined that the tire removal would cost $4,000. He called Jamie with the quote and, being empowered to solve the problem, she told him to go ahead and get it done. Within a few days, the tires were removed from Jeremy's property.

Jamie owned the problem and stayed in constant contact with the customer. I found out about the situation after it was handled, when Jamie mentioned it during one of our meetings. Spending $4,000 to fix it was not ideal, but the issue was resolved without me. That's flawless execution of the Outcome Delegation core need.

Now, you might be thinking, *I don't want my teams to have the ability to spend money unchecked.* I hear you. I want to approve certain things. But if we must fix something anyway, to me it makes sense to have automatic approval. I won't say that I agree with all the decisions made in these cases, but the misses become teaching opportunities. Nor am I advising you to bestow unlimited checkbook privilege. Jamie is one of my managers, so she has more latitude.

You can see this principle in practice in most larger companies. Take the Ritz-Carlton, the renowned hotel chain. They are known worldwide for their excellent customer service. One of the key factors contributing to their reputation is their famous $2,000 policy. It's simple: If an associate becomes aware of an issue that affects a guest, they can spend up to $2,000 to resolve it without needing manager approval. This approach empowers employees to ensure an exceptional guest experience and resolve issues immediately.

Empowered employees can prevent small problems from escalating, and it gives them the ability to delight customers without delay. Ritz-Carlton didn't just pick the $2,000 number at random. That amount came from understanding that the lifetime value of a Ritz customer is about $250,000. The Ritz management team also understands the psychological impact that quick problem resolution has on guests and their satisfaction. Another benefit to the program is that empowered employees have a higher job satisfaction. When your employees know that you trust them and their abilities, they like their jobs better.

It's also important to know that employees seldom use the maximum amount. In fact, they often use it on lower-cost solutions. During a stay at the Ritz in Naples, Florida, my wife and I went to dinner at their restaurant by the beach. With the sun still burning bright, we sat facing the water. My wife had forgotten her sunglasses in the room, and to shade her eyes she made a visor with her hand. Our server noticed and brought her a pair of Ritz-Carlton sunglasses. These were basic plastic glasses, but they did the job. Because this policy exists, I'm now able to share this experience with you.

Countless other guests have their own stories to share, from a server who brought kids Popsicles because of the heat, to an employee buying a guest's child a replacement for the beloved Thomas the Tank Engine that they'd left at home. The $2,000 policy positively impacts the Ritz brand, their employees' work satisfaction, and their clients' happiness.

As for Jeremy, my customer who bought the property filled with tires, he was impressed by our response. "I really appreciate the quick response and action taken," he wrote Jamie in an email. "Let me know if there is somewhere I can leave a review for you guys for the great service."

Empowering your team to make a difference and resolve issues quickly has a positive impact on your customers. The bigger benefit is that it's one less thing on your plate and one more reason your employees like working with you.

In the IPP, Order is about efficiency. The secondary benefit is creating a company that is less dependent on you.

ACRE: Outcome Delegation

IN THIS ACRE EXAMPLE, LET'S streamline the request process and empower the team. We want an engaged team that feels empowered to address problems without needing the owner's approval.

1. *Articulate the objective*: You and your team notice how many times your approval is needed to fix issues. Their requests interrupt your workflow, and waiting for approvals creates delays and bottlenecks. Empowering the team would mean fewer interruptions, faster resolutions, and happier customers. You and the team agree that the objective is to establish an approval threshold that doesn't require you to weigh in.

2. *Collect the metrics*: The team gathers and, after reviewing past financial decisions, discovers that 90% of all requests cost $500 or less. It's hard to imagine everyone having a $500 spend ability,

but the decision is made and the threshold is established. In passing, someone says, "Hey, we can always change it, let's try it."

3. **Rhythm**: It is agreed that every time the spending policy is used by a team member, they will log it in a shared spreadsheet. You also agree that this for now, this is a test and will run for three months. The goal is to see the number of owner approvals substantially reduced.

4. **Evolve**: You hold a meeting to announce the new policy and explain the $500 threshold. You encourage team members to take ownership of their financial decisions within that limit. You also provide training to help improve their financial decision-making abilities and encourage them to discuss these decisions with their peers when in doubt.

5. **Result**: After three months, you look at the results and can't believe it. The tracking document shows a 70% reduction in the number of issues you needed to approve. The team now makes decisions on their own and solves problems faster, resulting in happier customers and team members.

Also, you now have more time to deal with bigger-picture items. Or, better yet, you are one step closer to absolute time freedom.

CORE NEED #4: LINCHPIN REDUNDANCY

Question: Is your business designed to operate unabated when key employees are unavailable?

Recently, I was sitting in a hotel conference room in Santa Monica, California with close to forty entrepreneurs. As our meeting got under way, the moderator asked, "Who has had a great quarter?" Hands went up, and volunteers started sharing.

Sarah, one of the first to speak, told of her four-week summer trip to Ghana. "We had a great trip, made a ton of memories, and I didn't take a laptop with me, I left it at home. I didn't check my work email at all. It was the best trip ever!" The room erupted in applause, making me question, *Why is simply being able to take a vacation a win?*

This is an unfortunate reality for many of us. Research indicates that 67% of small business owners check in on work while they are on vacation. Even worse, 14% of owners only take a vacation every two to three years.[28] Ample medical evidence shows the negative impact that constant worrying about work has on your health. Overworking can lead to health issues such as heart disease, high blood pressure, obesity, and more.

The applause Sarah received in that hotel meeting room was well deserved because she beat the odds. In his book *Clockwork*, Mike Michalowicz discusses the need for owners to plan annual four-week vacations away from their businesses. This provides them with a healthy break, but it also forces their team to become more independent.

The four-week rule isn't just for the owner; it's also for key employees. One of the greatest challenges your business is likely to face is an overdependence on one or more employees.[29]

Bryce is a member of my team. He is not a leader, but he has an important role handling customer support for one of my companies. When he wanted to take a week's vacation, we arranged to have a backup in place, and Bryce did a great job documenting how every thing works. Despite lots of planning, we found things he handles that his backup didn't know how to do. Being a champ, Bryce still checked in while he was supposed to be enjoying time away. Each night he dove into the shared inbox, cleared out anything unfinished and, unlike a superhero, cleaned up the mess. His time away gave us a lot of insight. It is now clear that for many tasks, he is the linchpin, meaning that his role is so critical, he holds everything together.

How many linchpins do you have on your team? Are you a linchpin? What would happen to the business if you took off for a month?

These questions are critical to your independence and your team's. When you start out, you as the founder are responsible for everything. You wear every hat, answer every call, and complete every task. As the company grows and people join your team, you move into a leadership role but still feel the need to check on everything. Working through the IPP, fewer tasks are dependent on you. Our goal, after all, is recurring positive cash flows with very little active involvement. That can only happen if you share the work.

As I mentioned, Mike Michalowicz is a big proponent of the four-week vacation. When I was seeking his approval to write this book, his team informed me that he was unable to meet with me for over a month because he was on his four-week vacation. Amy, who works with Mike and to whom I also needed to speak, was finishing hers. These were not just words in a book; Mike and his team are the embodiment of this practice.

You cannot achieve time freedom if your business cannot operate in your absence. Now is the time to gather the team and announce your four-week vacation.

ACRE: Linchpin Redundancy

IN THIS EXAMPLE, WE WILL use ACRE to implement Mike's four-week vacation policy for the owner and all key employees of our investment company. This will ensure that the business operates smoothly and without dependence on any one person.

1. *Articulate the objective*: Realizing that your company is too dependent on you and a few other key team members, you implement the four-week vacation rule. This new policy requires all team members to take an annual four-week vacation. As the owner, you decide you will go first.

2. *Collect the metrics*: The team determines that the best way to measure the effectiveness of the program is to track the number of tasks that can be completed by multiple people. You've heard about cross-training? This is better. We're talking task redundancy.

    The team determines their goal: At least one other person should be able to complete 80% of a task in the employee's absence.

3. *Rhythm*: You commit to tracking the progress of the redundancy system over the next six months. Every week, the team receives an update on the number of tasks that have a qualified back-up.

4. *Evolve*: The implementation starts off rough. It becomes clear that a regular training program is needed. Every week, you walk the entire company through a key task and how you completed it. These sessions are recorded for playback if needed. You hand out playbooks that outline how work is done and other team

members test the steps, provide feedback, and ensure that the workflow improves with each iteration.

With the understanding that having someone gone from the business for four weeks will not come without some degree of pain, everyone agrees to be flexible during the first runs of the program and ready to answer help calls when necessary.

5. **Result**: After the six-month preparation period, you report to the team that 85% of your tasks can be completed by others. With the linchpin removed, you are ready to set off on your first four-week, work-free vacation. Prior to leaving, you give the team one last set of instructions. "If it's an emergency, don't call me—call 911. If it's a business emergency, please just fix it." So you aren't tempted to work, you leave your laptop at home, and to your surprise, your phone doesn't ring, not even once. You are able to enjoy your first true vacation as a business owner.

CORE NEED #5: MASTERY REPUTATION

Question: Are you known in your industry for being the best at what you do?

David Goldwasser, the founder and principal partner in FIA Capital Partners, is known for one thing: He's the go-to guy to work through complex real estate transactions. With experience in commercial and residential real estate, David knows his stuff. When a property gets into a distressed situation, such as with troubled loans or bankruptcy, he is at the top of the phone tree. He's the dude attorneys call first to see if he has an interest in the property.

While other investors are hitting the pavement looking for deals, David's deals come to him. And these are not small deals, either: They are large, notable properties like the Arlo Williamsburg Hotel and the Tillary Hotel, both in Brooklyn.

What gives David and his company the upper hand is their reputation for mastery. They are known for the exceptional work they do. Technically, they are known for their ability to solve problems. And because they are specialists, they have mastered their processes to create predictable outcomes.

Operating at that level makes growing a business much easier.

Remember Frank Rolfe, the fifth-largest mobile home park operator in the US? His company has also achieved a reputation for mastery. As a result, brokers flood their acquisitions team with off-market deals and they get the pick of the litter. They also use their mastery-level skills to refine processes, making acquisitions and improvement easier. Their reputation allows them to provide comfort for the residents of the communities they acquire. And they benefit from having a process or MO (*modus operandi*) that they can deploy when improving a community and to justify rent increases to residents.

My own company has achieved mastery reputation in our niche. As with David and Frank's companies, deal flow keeps getting easier, our processes become more streamlined over time, and the business can handle larger and larger deals. Another benefit of a mastery reputation is that you and your team know how to navigate both rainy and dry periods.

How can you achieve mastery reputation?

One thing that makes this core need difficult to fulfill is when investors bounce between real estate niches. I speak to so many investors who fail to gain traction in a niche or market because they are always looking for the next hot market or trend. Today they are flipping houses; next year they are moving into multifamily units. Mastery comes from working in the same market, industry, or niche for a while. The goal is to become the go-to firm in your market/niche.

This is where specialization comes in. In the Deal Flow-level Prospect Attraction core need section, we talked about the three stages of awareness and determined that stage three is finding your market. I shared the story of how my business gained traction by focusing on a 50,000-acre area in one county. When that happened, we sold more land, and our competition began referring customers to us when they didn't have specific properties available.

Specialization can come in many forms, including geography and type of property (land, multifamily, and so on). You can also specialize in a specific market segment, such as homes for first-time buyers, luxury properties, or, in the case of David Goldwasser, distressed properties. It can also be a combination of these, like distressed commercial properties in New York City.

Opportunities come when you have enhanced skills and knowledge in your area, which is what you gain from frequently dealing with the same types of transactions. You and your team master how to handle these transactions; it becomes second nature. Like an ER doc with their patients, you have a flow and you master that rhythm.

ACRE: Mastery Reputation

EXAMPLE TIME! IN THIS ACRE, you formulate a plan to build the reputation you deserve.

1. *Articulate the objective*: As the owner of Maximum Profit Real Estate, you recognize that your company has spread itself too thin by working in various niches and markets. The real culprit is DJS, Deal Junkie Syndrome, which is an STO (Scott Todd original). From residential flips to small multifamily units and a small retail strip center, you have gained exposure to many aspects of real estate investing. You enjoy new challenges but also realize that the niche you enjoy the most is residential property flipping.

2. *Collect the metrics*: You and your team commit to only dealing with residential properties for the next year. You establish a goal of fifteen flips per year with an average profit margin of 20%.

3. *Rhythm*: Every quarter, you share the metrics with the team. Are you moving in the right direction? Are you achieving the desired results?

4. *Evolve*: As the year progresses, DJS sets in and the team reminds you of your commitment. To support them, you arrange for training to enhance their skills in residential flipping strategies, market analysis, renovation techniques, and project management. Throughout the year, they become stronger as they learn to master transactions and processes and begin to move quickly through difficult situations. Because of the company's specialization, they have developed a flow.

5. *Result*: At the end of one year, you pull the team together and share the results. Because of your focused approach and their mastery of the niche, they successfully completed twenty flips and achieved an average profit margin of 23.6%. This improved overall profitability and established you as a reputable player in the flipping market.

TEAM ACTION: ACHIEVE ORGANIZATIONAL ORDER

ORDER IS CRUCIAL FOR CREATING efficiency and minimizing wasted effort. Here are some ideas for ways you can work with the leaders of the company to help them fulfill these core needs.

- **Find the bottlenecks**: Start by identifying the bottlenecks and areas that can operate better. You and your coworkers know right where they are. Where are the processes broken? Where can the workload be improved?
- **Document your work**: If you haven't done so already, building a playbook of the repetitive tasks you perform is vital. Those tasks that are completed once a month or less are the easiest to forget and the most critical to document. I know that when I have a task that I don't do daily, every time I do it, it's like having to start over. Documenting or building a checklist or playbook of how you accomplish such tasks will help you do them faster in the future.
- **Create the role you want**: I encourage you to be vocal about your role. You know your strengths and weaknesses better than anyone. If there is work that you would love to take on, I encourage you to step up and say, "Hey, I want to do that." The leaders of the company will appreciate your efforts. And better yet, you will help create the role you want.
- **Cross-train**: Cross-training is so important. It guarantees seamless operation in your absence and makes your work more interesting. And you get to learn about the work others do, which might spark your interest or curiosity, maybe even help you move your career in that direction. For example, you

might get exposure to accounting and realize that you want to learn more about it. Maybe it's your next role. You never know.

Chapter 6

FROM GETTING TO GIVING

WHEN BLAKE MYCOSKIE AND HIS SISTER WERE SELECTED AS CON-testants for the second season of the TV show *The Amazing Race*, he didn't realize the degree to which it would change his life, even though winning the grand prize of $1,000,000 would mean a totally different lifestyle for them. They didn't win; they finished in third place and missed out on the prize money. Still, the show led to an experience that transformed Mycoskie and the world.

The Amazing Race is a reality TV show in which teams of two race around the world. At each stop, they face various challenges that test both their mental and physical abilities. During the twenty-one-to-thirty-day competition, the teams are sent to different locations around the world. One of the stops on Mycoskie's adventure was Argentina. During the competition, there is no time to stop and experience the country. You are there for a limited time and then you jet off to yet another country.

After narrowly missing winning the competition, Mycoskie returned to his life as an entrepreneur.

In 2006, after closing his fourth company, Mycoskie needed a break from his entrepreneurial journey (remember when we talked about the lack of downtime in the last chapter?). As a type of sabbatical, Mycoskie chose to return to Argentina, but this time he wanted to immerse himself in the culture.

Mycoskie said, "I spent my days learning the national dance (the tango), playing the national sport (polo), and, of course, drinking the national wine (Malbec)."

The time away allowed Mycoskie to explore the country, traveling not just to the large cities but also experiencing what life was like in the countryside. While visiting one of the poorer rural areas, he observed that many people, especially children, were walking around without shoes.

He learned from a volunteer worker that the lack of shoes was a result of family finances. For these families shoes were a luxury, but they were a required part of the school uniform. Without them, the children were unable to attend school.

As he thought about the lack of shoes and how it affected the children, Mycoskie's entrepreneur mind activated. He realized that this was an opportunity. Rather than rely on charities to fill this gap, why not create a company with a social mission to do it? Mycoskie went on to create the shoe company TOMS. His initial goal was to provide 250 pairs of shoes for one town in Argentina. What came next exceeded his vision.

TOMS shoes rocketed to fame thanks to its buy one, give one (BOGO) program. When you purchased a pair of TOMS shoes, the company would donate a similar pair to a person in need. This product-based giving strategy allowed TOMS to scale quickly, thanks in part to the free press it received. Consumers connected with the company's mission and fueled organic word-of-mouth marketing. Its BOGO strategy set it apart from competitors, making it unique in the crowded shoe market. However, the very program that propelled TOMS to success soon revealed its flaws. As the saying goes, "No good deed goes unpunished," TOMS's giving program became a burden on the company.[30]

First came the negative publicity. The free shoes arrived in developing countries and began to disrupt local economies. As the donations flooded the market, local shoemakers saw a decline in demand. Complaints soared, eroding some of the goodwill TOMS had created. Talk about unintended consequences.

As TOMS's popularity continued to grow, competitors began to copy their shoe designs and the BOGO strategy. Less expensive knockoffs entered the market, leading to market saturation, which resulted in declining sales.

TOMS needed to support its BOGO program even as profits declined. As Mycoskie put it, "Giving is really hard."[31] What made giving at scale difficult was the resources the company needed to allocate to the program. A dedicated team supported the program, finding the areas in which to donate and handling all the logistics. These resources were not a burden on the company while it was growing. However, as sales declined, the overhead needed to support the program strained the company, contributing to its declining financial stability.

By 2019, TOMS was losing money and nearing bankruptcy. Mycoskie ran out of options and turned the company over to its creditors, allowing TOMS to avoid bankruptcy. The new CEO and management team eliminated the BOGO program. They chose to replace it with direct donations. The new program pledges up to one-third of the company's profits to charitable causes. Instead of donating shoes to developing countries, they donate funds to grassroots organizations that work on issues core to the company. In 2023, the company donated $1.7 million of its profits.[32]

The TOMS story exemplifies the importance of attending to your company's needs before turning your attention to giving programs. Your ability to impact your community and team members requires a strong foundation.

THE GETTING AND GIVING LEVELS OF THE IPP

THE IPP IS STRUCTURED IN an interesting way. Of its five levels, the three bottom levels—Deal Flow, Profit, and Order—form the Getting part of the framework. These foundational levels are essential to the long-term stability of the business.

Deal Flow is concerned with the creation of cash needed to operate the company. Profit supports the creation of stability in the organization. Order is about the creation of efficiencies that support the lower levels.

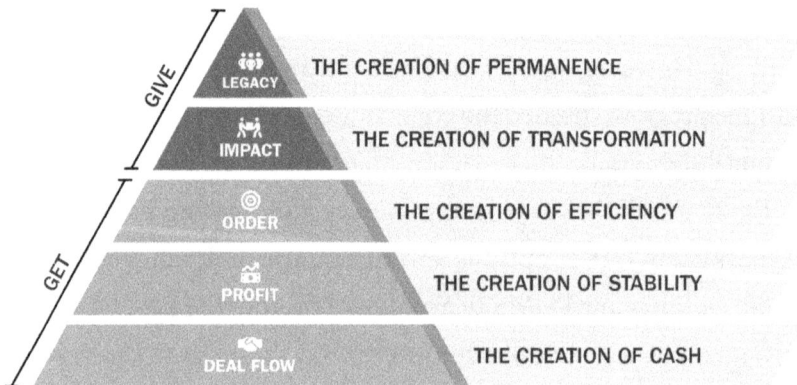

Figure 10: IPP with Getting and Giving Levels Identified

Every company needs to master these core levels. We need to get all of these resources in place before we can move higher in the IPP. As we saw from the TOMS story, if your foundation is weak, you cannot contribute at higher levels.

Mark Frissora, the former CEO of The Hertz Corporation (now Hertz Global Holdings) and Caesars Palace, told me, "I take care of myself first, my family second, and my company third. If I don't take care of myself, I'm of no use to the other two."

The practical value of this "me first, others second" mindset presents itself in so many situations.

My wife and I decided to purchase a boat, but she had one request: We had to take a boater safety course. I agreed and in lightning speed, I had us registered for a Coast Guard class the following weekend. The class covered all aspects of boat ownership; however, one of the most important parts of the weekend was the safety training. One of the more memorable moments for me was when they showed us how to handle a man overboard situation.

When a person is overboard or in distress in the water, the first thing to do is toss them a flotation device. The technical term is a "type IV throwable device" which, according to the Coast Guard, must always be immediately accessible and available for use. Man, did that training pay off.

The throwable is typically a square or ring buoy and is meant to supplement a life jacket to support someone in distress. It also can serve as a beacon in the water, showing you which way the current is moving and making it easier to find the person who has gone overboard as you turn the boat around. The second step is to put on your life vest. Ideally, everyone on the boat grabs a life vest. Yep, rule number one is that you do not help someone in the water if you are not wearing a life vest yourself. Doing so puts you at risk.

My boat safety training was tested a few months later when I was out on the boat with my wife, daughter, and eleven-year-old son. My son was behind the boat, enjoying some good old-fashioned tubing. As I turned the boat, he drifted outside its wake and the tube caught another wave and flew a few feet into the air. This sent my son flying off the tube and slamming into the water, and the impact looked rough; as I turned the boat and approached him, I noticed that he was visibly upset. He was floating upright thanks to his life vest but having a hard time swimming toward the boat. With the boat turned off and dad mode on, I jumped into the water. My suspicion was right; he was fine, just had the wind knocked out of him. Safely back on the boat, the day of fun over, we headed back to shore.

As we drove home talking about the day, my wife gently reminded me, "You didn't put your life vest on."

"What?"

"When you jumped in the water, you didn't put on a life vest."

"Yep, that's true."

Despite training and knowing what to do, in a moment of seeing another in need, I forgot the most important safety rule. Protect yourself first, because you are no help to others if you are also in harm's way.

Get the deals flowing, realize some profit, and get everything in order. These are the primary objectives of the company, and there is nothing wrong with prioritizing what it, your team, and you need. You are creating sales and profits because of the value you generate for others. Without value, your business wouldn't be able survive for long.

After you have satisfied all the core needs of the first three levels, then and only then can you transition into the world of giving. If you try to give while still in the Getting stage, it will weaken your business.

WE WANT TO HELP OTHERS

I'M SURE THIS WILL NOT surprise you, but as a human, you have a strong desire to help others. Research has shown that we tend to try and help others even if doing so will come at a personal cost.

According to a study published in *Scientific Reports,* someone signals for help every two minutes and seventeen seconds during everyday interactions among close social circles. This includes small requests like, "Can you pass a napkin?" The study found that people comply with these requests seven times more than they decline them.[33]

When we help others, we receive a psychological reward that further reinforces our altruistic behavior. We feel happier when we help others. It fulfills our social needs while creating meaningful experiences.

But it's also easy to neglect yourself when you try to help too much. As we discussed in the TOMS example and my boating story, giving at the wrong time can actually do harm.

TOMS's BOGO program did not directly cause the company's financial decline. However, from the outside, we can see how the program put a strain on the business that contributed to its instability. When TOMS should have been securing itself in the Getting levels of the IPP, specifically the Deal Flow level, they weren't. Because of the large commitment they made, they spent a lot of resources on giving.

TOMS is a great example of a company that needed to put their life vest on first but didn't. They are also an excellent example of a company stuck in the Giving phase when they needed to be getting.

When your business has Getting core needs to address, they come first. You can't allow Giving needs to impact your business. Giving is a good thing, but sometimes businesses never move beyond the Getting needs. That is OK, and it's also fine to give a little when you are in the lower levels. Yes, donate and support your community, but don't make it your purpose until your basic needs are met.

GIVING AND THE IPP

As you start to imagine what is next, the IPP is there to guide you.

Above the Getting levels, there are two more levels: Impact and Legacy.

Impact is about the creation of transformation in the communities we serve and in the lives of our team members. Legacy is about the creation of permanence. Here is where we challenge ourselves to think about turning what we started into something that will last beyond us.

The Giving core needs that are presented in the next two chapters are about so much more than simple donations. Here we will push you and your organization into a world that few investors ever consider possible. Master these core needs and you will have left your mark on the world.

Chapter 7

FROM TRANSACTION TO TRANSFORMATION

WHAT IF THERE WAS MORE TO BUSINESS THAN JUST PROVIDING for you and your team? What if there was a way to have a transformative impact on the lives of your customers, employees, and community?

I have conducted my fair share of vision-planning sessions designed to help investors build a three-year plan for their businesses and lives. During these sessions, I walk participants through each of the three years and have them identify where they see themselves in each period. What most people find is that around the two-to-three-year mark, their money and time freedom dreams are met, at least on paper.

Then comes the hardest question: "Then what?"

This is a true deer-in-the-headlights moment. Most people don't know what's next after they meet their goals. This is where we begin to ascend into the Giving levels of the IPP. But giving is not just about cash donations: It's about having an impact and creating a legacy through your business.

Many real estate investors reach a point where their business is running smoothly and become bored. Business coach Dan Sullivan once told me that the best skill an entrepreneur can learn is how to get good at being bored. But being bored is what leads investors to start looking at other types of real estate or get involved in other activities. Heck, it's why I learned to fly—I was bored. Similarly, this is what causes entrepreneurs who sell their companies to experience a profound sense of loss and identity crisis. It's during this time that you find them on the golf course, turning to philanthropic activities, or starting their next business.

During my sessions, when a participant reached the dreaded "then what," question, they predictably grew silent. After a few seconds of mental processing, they end up creating some very powerful whys. Some are personal, like "I just want to sit on a beach in the Caribbean for a month and watch my children have fun." Some are world-changing, like "I want to donate my time to fight human trafficking." Arriving at the point where we can think about life beyond our own needs is deeply fulfilling. We allow ourselves to tap into Maslow's self-actualization level and create a vision of our life's purpose as a result. Through my own achievement of this level, I too have been able to find my why. It is at this level that I found my voice as a teacher and trainer for entrepreneurs, showing them how to live their dreams.

In the rest of this chapter, we will explore the Impact core needs to create transformation in the world.

CORE NEED #1: TRANSFORMATION ORIENTATION

Question: Does your business benefit clients through a transformation beyond the transaction?

Remember the boating class my wife and I attended? The class took place in the conference room of Bass Pro Shops, the big box retailer that specializes in all kinds of outdoor products.

They routinely make their space available to organizations such as the Coast Guard and others who provide training to the public. Thanks to that space being available, we were able to benefit from affordable training that could save lives.

We sat in the classroom and listened to the instructors tell us about all the safety equipment we needed for a safe boating experience. My wife made her list and when the class ended, she said, "OK, let's get our stuff." We headed over to the store's boating section. We crossed item after item off the list, debating a few, but in the end all the safety gear was loaded into our shopping cart. It was like the Coast Guard was in cahoots with the store. I'm sure the store knew that making their space available would lead to sales, but that wasn't their primary motive.

When I discuss this core need, I emphasize that at this stage in a company's development, we seek a higher connection with our clients. Bass Pro's choice to work with external organizations that provide valuable training goes beyond the transactional. This kind of approach is transformative not just for our clients, but also for the communities we serve.

In the Capital Attraction core need, I shared how J. Massey arranged meetups for people to play *Rich Dad's Cash Flow* game. Did he hope to attract investors? Yes, but he also served a higher purpose. He was teaching others about the benefits of cash-flowing assets.

In my business, our clients have access to a series of videos that help them with their next step after purchasing. These videos are not about onboarding, but to help them understand how they can fully utilize their properties in the future. In the Transaction Frequency core need section, you identified opportunities to generate incremental revenue. Part of that exercise was to look at your customers' journey and determine what type of services come before and after you.

That's how I determine other ways to add value for my clients: by investigating what comes after me and what they need to know. In a core need we'll cover later, Complementary Network, we'll talk about even more ways to add value for your clients.

But now it's your turn. What do your clients need, and how can you help them on their journey? Gather the team for a fun brainstorming activity.

ACRE: Transformation Orientation

IN THIS EXAMPLE, WE WILL explore how a multifamily investor who operates in a lower-income market can use ACRE to make a transformational impact on their residents.

1. *Articulate the objective*: The objective of this program is to empower the residents of the complex who have limited educational backgrounds. You as the operator have found a resident leader who is able to help other residents. Your vision is for this resident to facilitate discussions and accountability meetings with interested residents who enroll in online courses. The resident who facilitates the discussions will receive a $50 rent credit for each class they lead. Each month, a new class is offered and the residents can sign up and earn transferrable

college credits for each class they complete. Your goal with this program is to help your residents acquire skills, improve their job opportunities, and transform their lives.

2. **Collect the metrics**: To measure the success of this effort, the company will track the following metrics:

   - The number of students enrolled. The target is 10% of eligible residents.
   - The attendance rate at each accountability meeting. The target is 75%.
   - The percentage of residents who complete their courses. The target is 60%.
   - You will also monitor resident feedback.

3. **Rhythm**: The company will monitor the results quarterly and adjust the program as needed based on the desired goals.

4. **Evolve**: This strategy can evolve in many ways. The frequency of the regular accountability meetings can change as needed. To start, you authorize one meeting per week, but you are willing to invest in two per week if needed. When you realize that one of the challenges to the program is access to Wi-Fi, you invest in a common area Wi-Fi system that gives residents access to high-speed internet. As the program evolves, you arrange for guest speakers to encourage the residents and consider incentives for completion of the courses.

5. **Result**: After one year of operating the program, the feedback from the residents is better than expected. Although the participation rate was below the target at 7%, attendance at the meetings averaged 78% and the course completion rate was 75%. You notice that the residents have increased loyalty toward your community, and it appears that they take better

care of the property. Your service calls have also decreased, resulting in an increased profit margin. Surprisingly, fewer residents now terminate their leases, which increases your occupancy rate, and residents are more accepting of the annual rent increase. One interesting side effect is that the number of residents who pay late decreased after the personal finance class.

CORE NEED #2: MISSION MOTIVATION

Question: Are all employees (including leadership) motivated more by delivering on the mission than by their individual roles?

Why does your team come to work? Is it for money or the mission?

Employees choose to work with your company for three primary reasons: money, work quality, and love, or community. Although there may be other reasons, these are the top three. Let's look at each of them more closely.

1. *Money*: This is the most straightforward reason. Employees work for the financial compensation. Most likely, they are not emotionally invested in the company or the company's mission. They wake up every day and head to work for one reason—to pay the bills.
2. *Work quality*: These employees are driven by the nature of their work. The work they do is challenging and interesting, and they like the tasks they are assigned, probably because their leadership nailed the core need of Role Alignment discussed in Chapter 5.

3. *Love or community*: These employees feel a strong sense of belonging and community within the company. They love the company, its mission, and/or the relationship they have with their coworkers. It's in this category that we find those who are mission-motivated.

As you can tell, there is a hierarchy of reasons why employees work for a company, money being the lowest level and love or community the highest. Employees who work only for the money will quickly leave you for ten cents more an hour. But those who love your mission will stay and fight to make it a reality.

Our goal is to create an organization filled with mission-motivated employees, so the weak mission statement you throw on the wall to justify your existence won't work.

"Be the best in the eyes of our customers and employees" or "Be the undisputed marketplace leader" are weak—so weak that only Ryan Reynolds, who regularly pokes fun at corporate culture, would enjoy them.

When large companies establish their mission, the senior leaders go into their fancy boardroom and concoct the mission statement without input from those who actually have to deliver the services. The mission becomes some big, fancy statement shared at a town hall and printed on fancy posters to hang around the office. But what if it was different? What if you held a meeting and asked the team, "Hey, what's our big goal?"

This is what happened at one of my companies, Landmodo, which is a platform to list and sell properties. I asked the team, "Why do we do this?" As we discussed our why, we determined that we are in the dream business. We are making it possible for our buyers to find the property of their dreams, directly from the investors who list on the platform. Our mission unfolded in front of our eyes: "We make property ownership dreams come true."

Now we have a mission that the whole team can get behind. Every day, we wake up with a mission greater than just making money. We want to help make dreams come true.

Now it's your turn. What is the mission of your organization? What do you and your team wake up for? Is it money, or are you on a greater mission? When you meet this core need, your team no longer shows up just for the money; they do it because of the mission. The exact mission is up to you.

ACRE: Mission Motivation

IN THIS ACRE, LET'S LOOK at how a home-flipping investment company can fulfill this core need by creating a mission that engages the team and the people they serve.

1. *Articulate the objective*: The objective is to create a mission that centers service to others, not just profits. Your company aims to renovate and sell homes for the underserved affordable housing market. You and the team get together and craft the words that will not only guide your decisions, but also represent a vision you can all rally around. After many attempts, you agree on this statement: "Our mission is to transform neglected properties into affordable homes that foster community and stability." This is exciting because everyone knows from the start what type of property to search for and the end goal, that it must be affordable for and uplift the community.

2. **Collect the metrics**: To measure success, you again gather the team to determine what metrics will tell you if you are heading in the right direction. You identify the following metrics:
   - The number of homes renovated and sold as affordable housing. The goal for the first year is ten.
   - The average sales price vs. the comp price. The first-year target is 5% below market price.
3. **Rhythm**: Every quarter, you will review the metrics to ensure that you are on track, but also to identify ways to become more efficient so the targets can be increased.
4. **Evolve**: Getting the sales price consistently lower than the market price is a challenge, and doing it while maintaining strong profit margins is difficult. During regular team meetings, everyone is encouraged to do a thorough review of Chapter 4 in this book and challenge every expense. After you share the mission with key vendors, some of them offer to help by arranging discounts for those homes and getting creative with ways that they can further reduce the prices of their products and services. Maybe you gift them this book and encourage them to read the profitability section. You start an interoffice campaign focused on bringing down the cost of these homes, and every quarter you create new posters for the common areas with slogans like "Cut the waste, grow with haste!" and "Trim the spend, profits ascend!"
5. **Result**: After one year, you gather the team to review the numbers. You sold twelve homes as affordable housing for 9% below the market average, thanks to some creative real estate sale approaches, and the profit margin was right on target thanks to your "Trim the spend, profits ascend!" campaign.

CORE NEED #3: DREAM ALIGNMENT

Question: Are employees' individual dreams aligned with the business's grand vision?

Back in my corporate job, before my bosses changed, I asked Bob, my manager, "How are you are able to bring out the best in the people on your team?" It seemed that everyone who worked for him loved him, and his division always seemed to perform well as a result.

Bob said, "Some managers try to drive their teams to perform. That rarely works. It might for a few months, but it's unsustainable. The thing to know about people and work is that while they are here at work, they want to do their best. But work is not the most important thing to anyone. Their dreams and goals are."

As I walked back to my office, I started noticing the staff differently. While some of the computers had company logo wallpaper, most showed background images of family, dogs, vacations, and memories. The pictures on their desks were of the same, not company stuff.

My daughter is an educator and loves her job, loves her students, but the pictures on her desk are of her family and her dog. Employees are driven by their dreams and goals. Our goal is to align each team member's vision with the business's vision.

As the third-generation leader of his family business, Chad Johnson took over his family's glass bottle-manufacturing company at a pivotal point. Increasing competition was pushing their products into the world of commodity and it was becoming very common to lose customers over fractions of a penny in price. Another challenge for Chad was his labor force.

Workers who manufacture glass bottles don't have the best working conditions. Making glass is a hot and dirty job. Traditionally, the work was done by immigrants who would work for a few months and then move on to another job. The glass-manufacturing work was a steppingstone. Because of the grueling working conditions, Chad had to deal with a lot of employee turnover, and running a company where he constantly had to find and train new employees created a tough management environment.

Then Chad discovered the Dream Manager program, which is documented in the book *The Dream Manager* by Matthew Kelly.[34] Chad's biggest takeaway from that experience was that, as he told me, "Personal dreams play a crucial role in job satisfaction and productivity."

Chad started to implement the program, which included talking with his employees and identifying their dreams and goals. During these meetings, he discovered something interesting. Because the majority of the team were immigrants from Mexico, they wanted to learn English. Chad responded by hiring an English tutor who taught classes before and after each shift.

The employees' response was overwhelmingly positive. Not only did Chad cure his turnover issue; he also increased productivity. There was another metric that changed as well. Because of this program, employees began recruiting their friends and family to come work with them. As you can imagine, the recruitment cost per open position decreased.

Chad didn't stop there; he kept digging to discover their dreams and found out that many of his employees wanted to learn how to buy a house. To help, he arranged personal finance workshops to educate them on how to save for and purchase a house. The business had a transformational impact on the employees.

When Chad first told me about the Dream Manager program, I read the book and began putting what I learned into action. One afternoon, I had the pleasure of meeting two young men, Seth and Evan. These guys had their dreams dialed in. They wanted to learn business and investing. I thought, "Heck, I can help with that." Today, they are members of my sales team, growing and flourishing while also being supported in realizing their dreams. That is powerful.

When you know where your team wants to go, you can align the business to support them. However, you won't know what they want unless you ask. It's also important to create an environment that celebrates their accomplishments and achievements.

In Mike Michalowicz's office, he has a wall dedicated to his team members' dreams. Once per quarter, the team meets to share goals and intentions, which are then added to the wall. The wall and the ritual are designed to serve as reminders of the important connection between the company's goals and those of the employees, ensuring dream alignment.

It's these connections that transform people from employees who only work for the money into collaborators and contributors who love their coworkers and the company mission.

Now it's your turn to talk to your team and learn about their dreams and goals. From there, you can determine how best to align them with the goals of the business. Doing so will rocket you forward.

ACRE: Dream Alignment

IN THIS ACRE EXAMPLE, WE will look at RealWealth, an investment company, and how they can implement a dream alignment program within their organization.

1. *Articulate the objective*: Tim, the manager, began a series of employee meetings with the goal of understanding the dreams and aspirations of each one of them. In his meeting with Wayne, who worked on the accounting team, Tim discovered that Wayne wanted to learn more about investing, specifically how to evaluate deals, and maybe participate in one with the company. Wayne had some money saved, but not enough to do the deal by himself. And Wayne was not the only one; other employees had similar goals.

2. *Collect the metrics*: Tim determined that a great metric would be to track the number of training opportunities that were made available to each employee, the attendance rate at each class, and how many dreams were fulfilled as a result.

3. *Rhythm*: They decided to evaluate the numbers monthly to ensure adequate training opportunities for all who wanted them. If space was limited, more training would be made available.

4. *Evolve*: As the program got underway, it became clear to Tim that it was a success, even an opportunity to cross-train the team. Employees were exposed to new deals and opportunities on a regular basis. Tim decided on one deal and allowed the team to invest in the property. Now, instead of mere employees, they were partners in the deal.

5. *Result*: After the first year, the employees sourced two deals, one in which the employees and the leadership team used 100% of their own capital. The employees enjoyed the experience as investors in the project—and it turned out to be the company's most profitable deal. These are culture-changing experiences.

CORE NEED #4: FEEDBACK INTEGRITY

Question: Are your people, clients, and community empowered to give both critical and complimentary feedback?

It's 10:50 p.m. and I'm watching TV with my wife when the commercial break turns into the news teaser—you know, the short break before the news starts where they tell you the upcoming headlines? Tonight, as the anchors tease the news, I see an image of Eddie, the guy who is renting a mobile home I own. There he is on my TV, looking upset as usual. The anchor's voiceover says, "Residents of a mobile home park claim their drinking water contains cyanide." Yes, the cyanide that poisons people.

Now, Eddie is a piece of work. He is loud, vocal, and will exaggerate the truth to get his way. As I sat anxiously waiting for the story, it seemed like forever before it aired. When it did, there was Eddie, telling the news reporter how bad the park management was, how the water was contaminated, and that the park also had sewage problems.

As it turned out, Eddie was trying to cause a scene because he was about to be evicted from the park for failure to pay his lot rent. This was his Hail Mary attempt to try to get the park to forgive his late rent payment so he could stay.

It didn't work. The next morning, I received a call from the park manager advising me that Eddie had broken multiple park rules and trashed the park office, he was still behind on rent, and they were calling the sheriff on him for removal. She didn't mention the news piece, but I'm sure it was also a factor. She also mentioned that I was responsible for Eddie's late lot rent payments and I needed to bring $575 to their office immediately.

The next call I received was from Eddie, telling me how he had been wronged and was leaving.

While his claims about the cyanide were fake, he had raised a legitimate concern about the sewage system at the park being outdated, and despite sharing this with the management team, they ignored it. In fact, Eddie had become the outspoken leader of the park in a battle between the residents and the park management. The management didn't want to spend the money to replace the aging septic system. The corporate ownership team was unaware of the sewage issues until Eddie's news appearance.

Negative feedback from your customer is not fun, but when you are operating with feedback integrity, you are open to all feedback, positive and negative. You also operate in a world where you are open to negative feedback from employees. In most companies, receiving negative feedback from your employees is rare.

Research from Cpl Talent Evolution Group found that nearly one-third of employees feel uncomfortable sharing negative feedback with their managers. The study also showed that of all the reviews left on ranking websites by former employees, nearly half of them are negative.[35]

The best way to combat the negative employee reviews and keep your customers from contacting the news is to be open to feedback from everyone. Feedback is critical, it's an important voice, and you can utilize it in your real estate investments to scale. We all know you can't make everyone happy; however, having open lines of communication is a great opportunity to learn from mistakes and grow in the process.

How do your customers and employees give you feedback? Larger companies tend to use customer and employee surveys. Although data tracking this does not currently exist, of the investors I have polled, very few conduct these surveys. Those who do target customers and ignore their teams.

Putting customer surveys into place is an important first step toward fulfilling this core need. One of the easiest customer surveys you can deploy is the net promoter score (NPS) rating. NPS was created in 2003 by Fred Reichheld, a partner at Bain & Company.

The concept is simple. Ask your customers one specific question and let them rank you from 0 to 10. Here's the question: "On a scale of 0 to 10, how likely are you to recommend our company to a friend or colleague?" Anyone who gives you a 9 or a 10 is a promoter and likely to tell others about it. Anyone who gives you a 7 or an 8 is a passive, meaning that they are unlikely to promote your business to others. Those who give you a 0 to 6 are your detractors. Their scores indicate that they weren't thrilled with their experience and are inclined to tell others.

The NPS formula is NPS = percentage of promoters minus percentage of detractors.

Let's calculate a NPS together. Let's say you have twenty surveys. Fifteen are promoters, two are passive, and three are detractors. Based on these numbers, your promoters are 75% (15/20) and your detractors are 15% (3/20). Therefore, in this example, NPS = 75 – 15, or 60.

Any positive score is good; however, above 70 is world-class. A negative number is a bad score and indicates that your company has several service delivery issues to address.

The NPS score alone will not give you qualitative feedback, meaning it won't give you the words that describe how customers are feeling. But adding a comments section to the survey will give your customers a greater opportunity to express themselves.

Now we need to shift to our employees. An easy first step is to implement a pulse survey. Pulse surveys are usually short, composed of five to ten questions that can be answered on a 1–5 scale, and often conducted on a quarterly basis. Here is an example of five questions that can be used in a pulse survey:

Using a 1–5 scale (with 1 being "Strongly Disagree" and 5 being "Strongly Agree"):

- *Job satisfaction*: I am satisfied with my current role and responsibilities.
- *Work-life balance*: I feel I have a good balance between my work and personal life.
- *Support from manager*: I feel supported by my manager to succeed in my job.
- *Professional growth*: I have opportunities to grow and develop within this company.
- *Engagement*: I feel motivated and engaged in my work on a daily basis.

As with the NPS, you should consider adding a comments section in your survey that will enable you to capture more details about how your employees are feeling.

NPS and pulse surveys are just two options to help fulfill this core need. With your team, brainstorm other options and create data collection methods that align with your goals.

ACRE: Feedback Integrity

IN THIS EXAMPLE, WE WILL use ACRE to implement a "Fix This Fast" program. The idea behind Fix This Fast is to create a webform on our company website that allows customers and employees to submit issues they would like looked at. This system will make corporate management aware of situations even when the local management team is not communicating them up the chain.

1. *Articulate the objective*: The objective is to have a process that allows customers and employees to report issues about the properties, services, or their overall experiences. This system will ensure that customers' voices (and the voices of team members, since they are internal customers) are heard by the corporate management team. The goal is to have a 90% response rate within forty-eight business hours.

2. *Collect the metrics*: The company will track the number of submissions and how long it takes for a member of management to address each one. The metric is the response rate.

3. *Rhythm*: Every week at the team meeting, the metric will be reviewed by the leadership team.

4. *Evolve*: The company creates an escalation team to address these concerns so the job of responding doesn't fall to the leaders. This prevents a bottleneck in responses or a linchpin situation. The escalation team has role alignment, so the right people are on the team. They also have outcome delegation so that they can fix the issues.

5. *Result*: By the end of the first year, the company has received seventy submissions and achieved a forty-eight-hour response

rate on 93% of them, exceeding the goal. And even better, they completely stayed off the TV news.

CORE NEED #5: COMPLEMENTARY NETWORK

Question: Does your business seek to collaborate with vendors (including competitors) who serve the same customer base to improve the customer experience?

After closing on his property, Robert Anderson called our office and asked, "Who can I use to have a survey completed?"

Jamie said, "Oh, you should call Dave Narrow, he's an awesome surveyor. Here's his phone number."

A couple of days later, Robert called again, this time asking who could install a well. Again we were able to provide him with the phone number of a vendor.

Being able to help solve your customers' issues is a powerful and unique differentiator. As you grow and refer more customers to your trusted vendors, you will often find that a complementary network evolves. These networks help businesses continue to grow organically.

But a complementary network goes beyond great vendors in your Rolodex. Everyone can be in your network, including those you would call your competitors. It's easy to see competitors through the lens of scarcity: If they get that property or that sale, I lose. But through the lens of an abundant mindset, you gain a new perspective.

Investor Andrew Dunn says, "When you're friends with investors in your market, you'll get deals without even trying: Ballers will offer you quick capital so you can do big deals, smaller investors send you leads they can't handle, and a grizzled veteran of real estate might mentor you."[36]

That mindset is important to your growth as an investor. As engineer, physician, and entrepreneur Peter H. Diamandis explains, "One of the most critical assets in the business world today is your mindset—how you think about your business, your company, your family, and so forth."[37]

When it comes to having an abundant mindset, investors Tri and Quynh Vu are a shining example. The Vus have made a practice of routinely traveling to meet up with other investors who should, by all intents and purposes, be considered their competitors. Jumping on a plane and flying from California to Florida to network or spending a weekend in Texas with other investors is not out of the question for them.

When I asked why they are so willing to spend time with their competitors, Tri said that "We do it for abundance… we just don't want to live in that scarcity mindset."

Beyond the abundance mindset, Quynh pointed out that while they do technically compete with other investors, they have also become friends with a shared interest. They are intentional about whom they connect with and actively seek out only those individuals who share similar values and goals. Having an internal network of people with similar business interests is also powerful as it provides them with an exit strategy. Through their network, they have been able to engage in partnerships such as wholesaling opportunities with peers they know and trust.

The Vus also see these interactions with their peers as instrumental to their personal and professional development. By adopting an abundance mindset, intentionally building relationships, and fostering collaboration, the Vus have created a complementary network to add to their arsenal of tools.

Think of a network as a form of ongoing education or a group of peers who can help you through a difficult situation. "Network" can also mean an actual network, as in TV network. Think about how many investors have grown their business to include TV coverage. The reality is that not everyone or every niche will end up on TV. Can you imagine how boring a land flipping show would be? Here's a picture of my dirt before and a picture of the dirt after.

The fulfillment of this core need requires that your business have a system in place that helps you continue to expand your network. It's through this network that you will make an impact on your customers, your vendors, your competitors, and the world.

ACRE: Complementary Network

IN THIS ACRE, WE WILL look at how your investment company can introduce a complementary network by setting up a "Preferred Providers Program" called "Scott's List" after your favorite author.

1. *Articulate the objective*: The primary objective is to establish a network of trusted service providers for your clients, vendors, and heck, even your competitors.
2. *Collect the metrics*: To measure success, you decide to track:
    - The number of providers. The goal is to have a list of thirty preferred providers.
    - The satisfaction rating of each vendor. The goal is an average satisfaction rating of 90%.
3. *Rhythm*: For the first year, you decide to track the progress monthly to make sure the results are in line with the targets.

4. ***Evolve***: To evolve this project, you establish clear criteria for the selection of a preferred provider. You determine that a key element is having regular communication with the preferred providers to ensure that they are able to support your clients and any other users of Scott's List. You also create an education program to promote the list to your clients and your network, emphasizing the quality and reliability they can expect. Additionally, you implement a feedback loop system so that users can share their experience and rate the vendors, which will help to alert you if the quality of a vendor's services has changed. If a vendor drops below the satisfaction threshold, they will be removed from the list.

5. ***Result***: Within the first year, Scott's List is a hit, with twenty-five preferred vendors and a satisfaction rate of 90%. Your clients love how you support them after the sale, and they reward you with referrals, deal flow, and sales leads.

FIX THIS NEXT IN ACTION

ONE OF MY FAVORITE STORIES from *Fix This Next* is Mike's explanation of how the Savannah Bananas baseball team has implemented the Fix This Next system. I found it very interesting to read about how they fulfilled their Impact needs.

"The ultimate privilege I experience as a business author is to watch the trajectory of a reader's entrepreneurial journey over the years. For me, the journey of Jesse Cole and his team has been top banana for me. His team takes all the bananas in the bunch… the Savannah Bananas.

"I first heard of the all-star league baseball team when the owner, Jesse, contacted me. He had read the first edition of *Profit First*, implemented it in their business, and because of his commitment to the profit process and to doing what others in the industry don't do, the Savannah Bananas have experienced unheard-of success. They have sold out the entire season for 2017, 2018, and 2019, and all indications are that 2020 is sold out and tracking to be their best fiscal year ever.

"I have been to multiple games and had the honor of throwing out the opening pitch during one of their games in 2018. In true Savannah Banana wacky style, the baseball was swapped for toilet paper (Jesse's homage to my first book, *The Toilet Paper Entrepreneur*) seconds before I walked out to the pitcher's mound. The dozens of hours of pitching practice did not pay off.

"Jesse and I have become friends. We have broken bread together, enjoyed many a long conversation, and Krista and I have even spent a weekend at his home on Tybee Island, Georgia. Jesse has also become a willing guinea pig for any new entrepreneurial tools I develop. So it is no surprise he was one of the first business owners I approached with the Fix This Next analysis.

"To set the stage (cough... baseball field), in 2019 the Savannah Bananas baseball team surpassed $3.5 million in revenue and had twelve full-time employees and 150 part-time employees. They led the league in attendance, revenue, profit, and countless other categories. Jesse went through the analysis and was able to check off all the needs at the Deal Flow, Profit, and Order levels. As he went through Impact, he triple-checked the Transformation Orientation need. There is no question that he was delivering baseball games; he was giving families clean, no-screen fun time. They are truly transforming families' and peoples' lives.

"As Jesse finished running through the Impact level, there was one box he couldn't check: Complementary Network. He had made progress in that area, but it was incomplete. So, Jesse got to work. First, he defined the outcome he wanted, and he looked at one great success he had already achieved in this category: beer.

"Jesse is in this business for the long term. He wants to extend the brand and grow it outside the confines of the stadium. If he squeezes people in with a shoehorn, maybe he could somehow expand attendance from four thousand to five thousand people. Jesse knew his ability to impact people in the stadium was maxed out, but if he could extend the brand outside the confines of the stadium, he could transform far more lives. He figured out the pathway to do this was through complementary vendors.

"Jesse had struck a deal in the prior year with the Service Brewing Co. in Savannah, Georgia, to brew the Savannah Bananas Beer with no royalties. The brewing company did not need to pay for the logo or name, they just had to make and can the banana-flavored suds and sell them at the games. The brews flew off the shelves. Service Brewing Co. had an instant hit on their hands, and the baseball team had another way people were experiencing the Savannah Banana culture.

"That's when it hit him... or better said, that is when it opened his eyes to what was right in front of him: TV exposure.

"Because of the Savannah Bananas' uniqueness, a regular stream of TV programs showcased the team. ESPN continued to feature them more than any other minor-league or all-star team. Jesse said, 'I realized we could leverage not just a complementary network, but a literal network.'

"With his Vital Need pinpointed, Jesse didn't need to pick up a phone and cold-call. He looked through all the past requests that had come in and vetted them. In the stack of media inquiries, there was a note from a company called Imagine Entertainment.

"Jesse returned the call as the baseball season came to a close. For the final two games of the 2019 season, Jono Matt, a producer from Imagine Entertainment, was sitting in the stands and taking it all in. He wrote up a pitch for a sitcom. If you have ever seen *Arrested Development*, think that, but with baseball.

"Of the 4,500 different pitches that have come to Imagine Entertainment, twenty have been selected for further development. And only one of them had a unanimous vote as the number one top choice to develop. Yep, you guessed it… the Savannah Bananas.

"The story will play out while this book goes to print, so you and I will see on the other side whether the show materializes. That said, it has a real shot. It has a real shot of changing millions of lives. And it has a real shot because the owners of Imagine Entertainment are Brian Grazer and Ron Howard. The gents who created *Arrested Development* and some of the greatest movies and TV shows of modern times.

"The Savannah Bananas are on the brink of radically extending their impact because Jesse pinpointed his company's Vital Need and concentrated his energy there. Wouldn't you know it, when something comes into focus, sometimes you find out it has been sitting in front of you the whole time."[38]

TEAM ACTION: DRIVING IMPACT TOGETHER

IN THIS TEAM ACTION, WE will look at ways that you can support your company in fulfilling the impact level needs of the organization.

The impact level is about creating transformation for clients, your community, and you, the team member. The purpose is to foster deeper connections with and loyalty to the company. You play a vital role in helping to achieve these impact level core needs. As a starting point, here are some actionable strategies you can use as a starting point.

The Transformational Orientation core need is about finding ways to create value for others beyond the transaction. You play an important role in creating this value. For example, Janet, who worked with a home rental investor on their leasing team, created guides and webinars that helped educate new tenants on what to do next after the lease was signed. These guides included school contacts, utility startup instructions, even introductions to their neighbors. What can you do to create value beyond the transaction?

When I covered the Mission Motivation core need earlier in the book, I used the example of my team's drive to create a platform that allows buyers to find their dream property. It's not a goal, it's our mission. Here's an important question that you and your coworkers should ask at this stage: What impact do we want to make on the world? Answer this question and I promise that the way you see your work will change. No longer will you be focused only on the money. You will have a higher purpose that improves your work environment.

When looking at how you can support the Dream Alignment core need, you should consider these questions: What do you want to achieve? What are your goals? Now's the time to be honest and figure out how they align with where the company is going. Consider establishing a dream wall in the office where everyone posts a picture of their next big goal. Maybe you put a picture of a house there. One of your coworkers might add a college degree, another a car. Then, as the dreams are achieved, hold celebrations where they are taken down and new goals are added. If you are virtual, do it with an online whiteboard or other tool.

Accepting feedback can be uncomfortable, and we confront it in the core need of Feedback Integrity. No matter how hard you try, you and your coworkers will miss things. However, being open to accepting feedback from others is critical to improvement. We all have room for improvement. The same applies to organizations. Internally, managers will provide feedback on your performance. Feedback from external parties such as customers and vendors will help you see areas of the company that are not working as they were intended. Receiving the feedback and acting on it will improve processes and experiences. Consider ways you can help. Maybe you can create an organizational system to maintain the feedback. You can fix or suggest ways to fix the areas that others have identified as needing attention. Talking to your manager about how they think you can help also makes a big difference.

Building a complementary network of people is hard. The more people who participate in identifying partners or vendors for the company, the easier it gets. It's OK if you don't feel comfortable building connections on your own. However, if you see opportunities that might make sense for your company, speak up. Share the details with a manager. What other ways can you help build a complementary network?

Chapter 8

LEAVE YOUR LEGACY

IN MASLOW'S THEORY, THE TOP LEVEL IS SELF-ACTUALIZATION. Here you can be the best version of yourself, doing what you love. Legacy represents the highest level in the IPP, where your company can realize its full potential and focus on creating permanence and serving future generations of customers and employees.

My business partner Mark Podolsky and I were talking one Saturday morning about weekend plans, upcoming vacations, and life in general, and then Mark asked, "What's our exit plan? Private equity?"

"That's not how I see it," I replied. "I see our company as something that lasts forever. You and I get replaced by future partners, who are replaced by future partners. We create a legacy."

Mark was surprised. He said he had never considered that an exit plan but liked it. I added, "We are playing an infinite game, not a finite one."

When most investors start, they focus only on meeting their personal goals. Most investors rarely think beyond the Getting phase, and if they do, fulfilling core needs above Impact is even rarer. But for those investors who venture into this Legacy level, the journey takes on a whole new meaning.

I debated writing this chapter because most investors don't make it here. According to Maslow, only about 2% of people reach self-actualization. I estimate that about the same number of investors achieve the level of Legacy. But real estate is all about legacy. One of the cornerstones of legacy wealth is cash-flowing properties left for future generations. We can see what might be possible with all the lower levels achieved. Like reaching the pinnacle of the mountain, at the Legacy level, we see the world from a different perspective. From here, we can create new dreams and goals that are greater than we had envisioned. This level of the IPP is where the infinite game concept challenges us.

Games can be categorized into two types: finite and infinite. Finite games have established rules, start and end times, and you keep score. You can also tell who is winning and who is losing, and at the end you declare a victor. These games can be formal or informal. You can make them up. Did you ever make up a game with your friends as a child? I did. We just made up the rules. You would get a point for touching a certain tree or hitting a ball past a particular point. To play a finite game, you have to agree on the point system and the rules. Every sport meets these criteria.

Infinite games are different. First, there are no rules. They lack a starting time or ending time, you can join at any time, and you don't lose unless you quit. Keeping score is impossible; you could define metrics that show how you rank, but maybe your competitors rely on a different measurement of success. I laugh when a business declares that it is the best in its industry because of its customer service score or other vanity metrics. Who agreed on that metric as the determinant of success? Business, international trade, personal growth, and health are a few examples of infinite games.

Infinite thinking gives us more time to achieve our desired results. Entrepreneurs love the word "scaling." We want to scale by a factor of ten or, more realistically, achieve our goals faster. We create aggressive goals built on artificial time horizons, creating a false sense that is where we should be. Then, when we don't achieve our goals, we become disappointed and critical of our progress. But we should be proud of how far we have progressed when we look back at our progress instead of measuring it against artificial goals.

Infinite thinking helps reduce the fear that consumes so many investors and paralyzes us, preventing us from acting. One of the fears a real estate investor faces is, *What if I can't sell this property in the future? What if I'm stuck with this property?* If you are playing with an infinite mindset, such thoughts disappear because, at some point, all properties will sell.

Danny Bradford owns twenty-four properties, including gas stations, retail spaces, and land. In 2004, he purchased a 1.7-acre commercial lot for $68,500. He's committed to holding the property until it sells for $300,000. Every few years, he lists the property with a realtor and sets a firm listing price at his target. Through the years, he has received many offers, never at his asking price.

I asked him, "Why won't you sell for less?"

"I will get my asking price at some point in the future," he told me. "If I don't, my children or grandchildren will; either way, my family will get it."

I broke out my financial calculator when I heard Danny's story and started punching in numbers. *Holding period, thirty years, purchase price, sales price, computer yield—5% per year? I can do better than that.* While other investors play a finite game focused on the shorter-term or vanity metrics like yield, Danny has a different mindset. He's playing an infinite game focused on legacy.

The rest of this chapter will challenge your thinking, giving you a view of a future you couldn't conceive of before. It will outline ways to fulfill the core needs of Legacy.

CORE NEED #1: INTENTIONAL LEADERSHIP TURN

Question: Is there a plan for leadership to transition and stay fresh?

Frank, a friend of mine, once asked me, "What happens to the business if something happens to you and Mark?"

"We operate like the president and vice president of the United States. We don't travel together, so the odds of something happening to both of us at the same time are slim," I answered, thinking that was the end of the conversation.

"Great, but what if something did happen?"

"We have Tate!" I replied. "Tate Litchfield works on our team, and he can step into our shoes tomorrow with no issue. And beyond that, Tate is working to train the next generation of leaders to cover for him."

If you work with capital partners or investors, you may have heard a similar question. Whether you call it a succession plan or an intentional leadership turn, preparing for a new generation of leaders is a smart strategy.

A group of family investors faced a similar situation. Three brothers began investing in property in 1985. At one point, they owned more than 9,000 properties, but forty years later, they faced a foreseeable problem: Who would run the business as they retired? In their hearts, they wanted their children or their spouses to step up to lead the family business, but no one did.

This investment group is not alone. According to a Businessweek. com study, "About 40 percent of U.S. family-owned businesses turn into second-generation businesses, approximately 13 percent are passed down successfully to a third generation, and 3 percent to a fourth or beyond."[39]

Now that the brothers are ready to retire, they struggle with their exit strategy. While the answer might seem simple—sell the business—they don't want to. Elliot, one of the brothers, told me, "Selling would mean the end of our life's work."

You might ask why they didn't hire a leadership team or why they don't do it now.

Elliot said, "We should have brought in a leadership team years ago, and we didn't. It was a mistake." Today, they feel that the process of establishing a team would take too long, and fear that their options are running out.

Leadership turnover affects all businesses, small and large. Most smaller companies solve this problem by selling or shutting down. On the surface, large companies have it better. But they also struggle when changing leaders.

In February 2020, Bob Iger retired as CEO of The Walt Disney Company. He had a hand in choosing his successor, Bob Chapek. Chapek faced an immediate challenge: the global pandemic, COVID-19. The worldwide shutdown resulted in the Disney parks closing for months. This wasn't the only challenge he encountered. He was leading the company through a very challenging era. By all accounts,

Chapek is a talented leader, yet he struggled in his role. In November 2022, his old boss, Bob Iger, was again named the CEO, ending Chapek's run.

Disney is a solid example of a company's struggle to find a suitable CEO. It can be even more challenging for our investment firms. Most investors don't reach the point in their business planning cycle where they must consider how to handle succession planning. So many sell their assets, or their children do when they pass. One of the advantages larger companies have is their continuous recruitment efforts. Recruitment programs bring in new talent to replace turnover and support growth. Each new employee brings the company fresh energy, ideas, and excitement.

Within my own company, we are always looking to fill roles with an eye on their future potential. This type of position is a dream job for those hungry to learn about real estate investing. To fulfill this core need, you need a system to recruit fresh talent into the organization, allowing you to build your bench strength with future leaders.

ACRE: Intentional Leadership Turn

IN THIS ACRE, WE WILL build out our intentional leadership turn. The good news is that, since we have already completed the core need of Linchpin Redundancy, we have already done most of the heavy lifting.

1. *Articulate the objective*: The objective is to establish a clear line of succession; not just who's in charge if something happens to the leader, but what the next generation of leaders needs to do to be ready. To start, we ask everyone in the company to

identify their successor. Then we complete an analysis of who is ready and the areas everyone needs to improve on. With that information, we move on to development plans for the key successors.

2. ***Collect the metrics***: To measure success, we decide to track the following metrics:
   - The percentage of managers in the company who have identified a successor. The goal is 90%.
   - The number of employees who are involved in leadership training modules. The goal is for 80% of the identified people to be enrolled in a manager development program.

3. ***Rhythm***: To ensure that the program provides ongoing employee development, we agree to review the metrics semiannually.

4. ***Evolve***: The selected employees are enrolled in a series of ongoing training programs designed to round out their development. Some key leaders are provided with opportunities to attend executive education programs provided by major universities. The company also implements a mentorship program in which managers mentor the next generation, helping to transform them into future leaders.

5. ***Result***: After one year of the program, the company hits its goals. At the same time, turnover and our pulse survey results have improved.

CORE NEED #2: QUARTERLY DYNAMICS

Question: Does your business have a clear vision for its future and dynamically adjust on a quarterly basis to bring that vision to fruition?

In 2015, Ben Sullivan took over as the CEO of his family's real estate company. The company's revenues had plateaued at around $15 million annually for years. He assumed the role of CEO to replace his father, who had retired. With a team of nineteen people to run it, he thought that growing the company would be easy, but after six years of trying everything imaginable, revenues stayed flat.

Ben told me, "I was defeated. I turned to my father and said, 'Maybe this is as big as the company will ever be.'"

His father agreed.

But Ben wanted more. He wasn't willing to settle. Ben set off on a planning trip. Armed with a few sticky easel pads and his ideas, he headed to his favorite getaway spot a few hours away.

When Ben arrived at the hotel, he set up shop and got his working space in order. Then, on the first page of the pad, he wrote "Three-Year Goal" and "$30 million" in giant letters. The goal was to achieve this by the end of the third year, so he wrote that date at the bottom of the paper. Ben tore off and stuck the page to the wall so that it was as close to the door as possible; he would need lots of wall space for this project.

Ben wrote his starting point on the next page, "$15 million," followed by the current date. He placed that page as far to the left on the wall as possible. With the goal identified, Ben started at the end. Ben told me, "Begin with the end in mind, isn't that what Stephen Covey said?" He knew that twelve quarters were between the start and the end of the three years, so he created a page for each quarter, adding each one to the wall in the correct sequence.

There were now fourteen 25" x 30" sticky pages on the wall representing the starting point, the quarters, and the end goal. Ben said,

"There was so much paper, it didn't fit on the wall. I had to double up, placing one higher than the other."

Over the next two days, Ben built his battle plan for how he thought the business could move forward. For the first time since taking over from his father, he felt confident the plan would work. He also knew that this was his plan; the team just needed to accept it.

Upon returning to the office, he booked a conference room at a local hotel, grabbed his key managers, and repeated the exercise with them. This time, he let them build the plan while he moderated. What they created was a three-year vision for the company. Knowing that the best-laid plans must be dynamic, he booked the same conference room for the last week of each quarter. Having a scheduled off-site meeting forced his key team out of the office so that they could reassess their progress and create a new quarterly plan based on where the business was.

A key part of the off-site strategy included identifying their quarterly focus. The leaders agreed on the top focus for the quarter and created themes. These themes became common marching drums for the company, ensuring that everyone was aligned. Theme-centered posters were hung on the office walls, added to video conference backgrounds, and generally used to remind the team where they were going.

More importantly, the off-site meeting cadence helped them solidify the vision and turn it into a reality. The business grew in revenue, exceeding its target in two and a half years.

Ben said, "It happened because of our quarterly meetings. We knew what we wanted and had a system that allowed us to adjust dynamically each quarter."

Now it's your turn to create a quarterly plan.

ACRE: Quarterly Dynamics

IN THIS ACRE, WE WILL design a quarterly dynamics program for our apartment operation. Let's say we operate five complexes, each one being a separate business unit.

1. ***Articulate the objective***: The objective is to create a quarterly review process to evaluate the company's performance. This process will also consider market conditions to ensure that strategic initiatives align.

2. ***Collect the metrics***: The team decides to track the following metrics:
   - The completion rate of the active projects. The goal is for all projects to be on track for completion.
   - The percentage of complexes that meet or exceed their performance targets in the quarter. The goal is for 100% of the locations to meet expectations during the quarter.

3. ***Rhythm***: Because this core need is designed to look at quarterly performance, we decide to meet quarterly to review the last quarter and plan the next one.

4. ***Evolve***: We decide to have our quarterly planning meetings at an off-site location and, like Ben Sullivan, we book a meeting space at a hotel for two days at the end of each quarter. During the two-day meetings, the team conducts a thorough review of the last quarter and then identifies plans for the next quarter. Part of the planning includes looking at each of the five locations and creating a unique plan for each. The onsite managers use video technology to attend remotely during the planning

sessions. This gives them a voice in the creation of their bespoke plan. It also empowers them to determine the actions needed to execute the new plan. When the quarterly plan is in place, it's execution time.

5. **Result**: After one year, the company reviews its progress. We didn't hit 100% on our two metrics; each were in the high eighties. But we did have a stronger year because everyone was working toward a clear, unified goal.

CORE NEED #3: ONGOING ADAPTATION

Question: Is the business designed to constantly adapt and improve, including finding ways to better and beat itself?

Borders was an international bookseller that operated more than 700 locations. The company was not just a bookseller; they took great pride in innovation. Compared to their competitors, they had a superior inventory system, which allowed them to predict consumer patterns well before other retail stores had this capability. They were also about the customer experience. The company installed computers throughout the store that allowed customers to search for inventory and learn where to find it. The same computers permitted users to see inventory at other stores or order books that were unavailable in the store without interacting with store personnel.

Their innovations didn't stop with technology. They were leaders in customer experience and focused on how to better serve their customers. They were one of the first retail stores to partner with

Starbucks, bringing them into the store so that customers could grab their favorite drink and sit in the café to read, study, or socialize. The chain was on the cutting edge, adding CDs and DVDs to their stores before other booksellers copied them.

Despite all their forward thinking, Borders lacked clarity in one strategic area: digital book sales. Like the rest of the bookselling industry, Amazon changed how consumers purchased books, affecting all booksellers. In 2007, Amazon brought more change to this industry when they released the Kindle eReader. Not only could consumers buy books online, but now they could also buy digital books from a reading device. In 2009, Barnes and Noble answered the Kindle with the Nook. While there was an apparent movement toward online sales and digital books, Borders struggled to identify its path.

What made it difficult for Borders to move forward was their focus on the bookstore experience. The company believed that consumers wanted to go to the bookstore and spend time there, so they focused on perfecting that experience. What set them apart was their attention to detail in the store. They were known for having thousands of books at a location. A company focused on the in-store experience doesn't need to worry about online sales and digital books. But as sales slipped and profits plummeted, they realized that they were wrong. In 2010, they decided it was time to add online ordering, which they outsourced to Amazon. At the same time, they finally released their digital reader, Kobo.

But it was too late. The nail was in the coffin. Borders filed for bankruptcy in February 2011 and closed permanently later that year.

It would be easy to blame Amazon and its disruptive technology for Borders's downfall, but the more significant issue was its failure to adapt and improve. When most people think of disruption, they think of changing an entire industry, like how Uber changed the taxi industry. But great companies get good at disrupting themselves. They learn to adapt and improve.

While real estate investing fundamentals remain the same, technological changes and better access to data provide investors with new ways to improve processes and operate more efficiently. Those who don't adapt and improve will struggle in the future.

Changes in payment collection technology are one example. Some investors use tools that automate the collection of rents and payments, whereas others still collect payments manually or, worse, make their customers mail checks. Leveraging technology in this area is an example of adapting to change.

Fulfilling this core need requires a system that continuously looks for ways to disrupt your company before others can.

ACRE: Ongoing Adaptation

IN THIS ACRE, WE WILL look at how we can beat ourselves and improve in the process. We gather the team and start by explaining that we are about to run a scary but fun scenario. We announce, "We are going to shut down unless we change how we operate." After the team gets over the initial shock, it's time to get to work.

1. *Articulate the objective*: Our objective is to identify all the ways that we are not currently performing to our potential. We split our whiteboard into two columns, "Working" and "Not Working." The group will spend one minute writing what's working on sticky notes, using one sticky note for each item. Those notes will be added to the whiteboard on the Working

side. Then we repeat the process for Not Working. How can we adapt to improve upon what is listed in both columns?

2. **Collect the metrics**: To measure success, we decide to track:
   - The number of actionable insights generated from the Not Working category. The goal is twenty actionable opportunities per quarter.
   - The implementation rate of the identified opportunities. The target is a 75% implementation rate per quarter.

3. **Rhythm**: Every quarter, we will review our progress on improving on what's not working. We will repeat the Working/Not Working sessions, making improvements quarterly.

4. **Evolve**: Making the commitment to adapt or improve requires a regular cadence of activities. Starting with the initial brainstorming session, we repeat our practice quarterly so that we don't get stuck in our routine. Each quarterly session, we generate an action plan to implement the improvements. We determine that each quarterly session should include time to recognize and reward team members who contribute to and help implement the changes.

5. **Result**: After the first quarter, we gather to review our progress. Our team addressed twenty-five actions and implemented twenty, achieving the targets. More importantly, one of the initiatives improved customer satisfaction by 10%, whereas another lowered expenses by 5%.

CORE NEED #4: CLIENT COOPERATION

Question: Do you foster cooperation with and support for your clients in need?

Helen heard a knock at her door. She wasn't expecting visitors, and at ninety-three, getting to the door required extra effort. On her way there, Helen shouted, "Who is it?"

All she heard was a mumbled voice she couldn't make out. Through her peephole, she saw Rebecca, the manager of the mobile home park where she lives. Helen began trying to unlock the door. She was confused as to why the Rebecca was there on a Saturday; it must be important. Her hands shook a little as she turned the doorknob. *I hope everything is OK,* she thought.

Helen was greeted by a smiling Rebecca. "Hi, Helen, I have a surprise for you. We wanted to come out today and help you clean up around your house. We have people from our office, and your neighbors are here too."

Surprised, Helen replied, "I can't pay you for this."

"Oh, no, this is all for you. We want to help you."

To give back to his clients, Bryant Davis, the park operator, regularly organizes days of service for his clients. Each manager can nominate one person who lives in their community and whose home needs some TLC. Bryant and his management team choose the resident they would like to help.

The management team coordinates everything. Seventeen people work in Bryant's corporate office, and they mobilize as many of them as possible. They gather the local manager, vendors, and staff, even fellow park residents. They plan all the work they will complete and stage the supplies and tools.

The staff and volunteers meet at the park entrance, discuss their plan around coffee and donuts, and then get to work. The first order of business is to inform the resident of their plan.

Helen could not believe that so many people were there to help her.

The crews jumped into action and began executing on their plan to trim the trees and bushes back from the house, pressure-wash the home, and tear down and rebuild the ramp that led to the porch. In a flash, the quiet neighborhood was filled with the sounds of pressure washers humming, hammers banging, and chainsaws cutting. Music played by the volunteer crews was drowned out by all the other sounds.

Laughter and energy filled the air, bringing love and support to this lady in need.

A few times during the day, Helen stepped out on her porch, curious to see what was happening, and was greeted with much fanfare. Today was about her.

As morning turned to afternoon, the items on the to-do list were ticked off one by one. Finally, after all the debris was removed and the tools stowed out of sight, it was time for the reveal—time for Helen to see what they had done.

Rebecca knocked on the door again. "Helen, we are ready. Come out and see."

Helen stepped onto the porch with the support of her walker and was met by a round of applause. The people there for her applauded! She was the reason for this day, and they wanted to serve her.

Helen stopped and looked around. She couldn't believe her eyes. The first thing she noticed was the new ramp.

Helen exclaimed, "Oh my, this is so much better."

As she walked down the ramp toward the street, she saw that the overgrown hedges had been cut back. "I love how much light is coming through windows now!" she exclaimed.

When she arrived at the road, she turned back to look at her house. "It's so clean and beautiful."

Helen struggled to shout to the volunteers, "Thank you, all of you, my house looks so great. Now when my family comes to visit me in my final days, they will remember what a beautiful home I lived in."

The volunteers were rewarded by Helen's joy. Coming from humble beginnings, Bryant always knew that he wanted to make a difference to his community. Quarterly days of service are just one of the ways that he lives this core need.

ACRE: Client Cooperation

IN THIS ACRE, WE WILL look at implementing client support in our investment business.

1. ***Articulate the objective***: Our objective is to help tenants in need. Unlike other landlords who only care about collecting their monthly rent checks, we aim to be different. Understanding that our residents might fall on hard times from time to time, we want to build a team of both internal staff and external partners who can help residents in need.

2. ***Collect the metrics***: We will track the following metrics:
   - The number of clients we engage with to support. We aim to assist one resident per quarter.
   - The type of resources provided, including financial assistance, counseling, referrals to local services, and clean-up days.
   - The success rate of our efforts. Our goal is 80%.

3. ***Rhythm***: We evaluate this effort on a quarterly basis, and we are ready to adapt or improve the program as needed.

4. ***Evolve***: To move this project along, we connect with local non-profits and social services to understand the type of services

they provide. Then we educate our team on the best way to engage these services for residents in need. Part of the training program covers how they can identify who needs support and how to approach the resident to propose solutions. Hopefully our residents don't require support and services, so we shift our focus to building service days.

5. **Result**: During the first year, one resident needs assistance in covering their utilities payment. Our team assists the resident in negating a payment plan with the power company and engages a nonprofit to provide food benefits for a month. The additional support means that money normally allocated to food can be redirected to the utility bills. After one month, the resident is back on her feet. Additionally, we plan four service days to help residents. The team starts to clean the common area around homes and help as needed.

CORE NEED #5: LEGACY OF CONTRIBUTION

Question: Is the organization's impact recognized and amplified by individuals and organizations aligned with its values?

Edward J. DeBartolo Sr. began his real estate investing company in 1944. After World War II, he witnessed the move from urban to suburban living and identified the need for retail space in these areas. In 1948, he developed his first suburban retail shopping center, which became one of the first strip malls.

In 1951, DeBartolo expanded from the strip centers to major shopping centers, and he continued growing his company to thirty-one regional malls by the 1960s. Throughout his life, the company continued to grow; at one point, it owned or operated over a hundred malls encompassing more than 78 million square feet of retail space. It also controlled nearly one hundred million square feet of commercial office space. The company owned more than just real estate; among other things, it owned two professional sports franchises, the San Francisco 49ers and the Pittsburgh Penguins.

In the early 1990s, Bartolo Sr. positioned his son, Edward J. DeBartolo Jr., to take over the business. In 1994, DeBartolo Sr. passed away with his son in charge. During the same year, DeBartolo Jr. oversaw the transfer of the holding into a public real estate investment trust (REIT) and raised $560 million in its IPO. In 1996, DeBartolo Jr. oversaw the company's merger with Simon Property Group, creating one of the largest shopping mall operators in the United States.

With the family business now in the hands of a large publicly traded company, the DeBartolo family reached their "now what" moment. Sure, they could enjoy their lives flush with cash, but that's not what they wanted. They wanted to do more.

In 2001, DeBartolo Jr. and his wife and daughters established The DeBartolo Family Foundation with the goal of channeling "the same level of care, compassion and dedication that has allowed the DeBartolo family to find success in real estate, sports, and other ventures, into efforts that help serve the underserved communities of Tampa Bay." Now the family works in their foundation, distributing income to causes that align with their values.[40]

Fulfillment of this core need has allowed them to fund a state-of-the-art animal shelter, make annual scholarships to students, donate to school funds for teachers, and more. Now they can focus on making a difference in their community and leaving a legacy.

Dr. Phildra Swagger, an educator in Hillsborough County, Florida, wanted to establish a charter high school. She envisioned a school with an emphasis on providing high-quality education similar to what you would find in top-tier private schools, but available to the public at no cost. Swagger enlisted her friend, former professional football player Derreck Brooks, to help. Brooks turned to the DeBartolo Family Foundation for funding. In 2007, the new school, Brooks-DeBartolo Collegiate High School, opened thanks to the support of the foundation. Because of their support, Swagger calls the foundation "the school's 'silent financial angel.'"[41] This is one of the countless projects the foundation has funded.

Legacy is the ultimate form of impact we can have. Fulfilling this core need takes a lot of work over decades; DeBartolo Sr. started his business in 1944, and the foundation wasn't established until 2001. Looking at this family's multigenerational story, you can see how they moved through all levels of the IPP and fulfilled each core need. Today, a third generation of DeBartolos leads the foundation, ensuring its ability to sustain its legacy in perpetuity.

ACRE: Legacy of Contribution

IN THIS ACRE, WE WILL explore how we can use our land investing experience to acquire land at below-market value and donate it to low-cost housing organizations like Habitat for Humanity.

1. *Articulate the objective*: Our objective is to create a structured program that continuously provides support for our selected organizations.
2. *Collect the metrics*: We will track two metrics:

- Organizations we support. The goal is three.
- Properties acquired for the cause. Our goal is twelve per year.

3. **Rhythm**: We will evaluate our progress annually.

4. **Evolve**: Our program will require coordination with the home building organizations. The first step is connecting with them to understand what areas they are looking to build homes in and what the target properties look like. With this knowledge, our teams can begin working their magic. When a property meets the guidelines, we present it to the organization. Once closed, we transfer the property to the organization to do what they do best. Because our mastery is in land acquisition, we stay true to that focus and allow the builders to do the rest. One by one, we continue acquiring properties and doing our part to help these important organizations.

5. **Result**: When the first year is complete, it's time to celebrate. We achieved our goal of helping three organizations to build twelve houses. The impact is felt by the recipients of the homes and by the members of our team. When each new homeowner moved in, the team contributed to a personalized gift for the family. Not only do we feel great about our contribution to our community, our team knows that they are making a difference, too—and that's Legacy.

TEAM ACTION: LEAVE A LEGACY

YOU CAN IMPACT THE LEGACY of your company. From where you are sitting right now, you may not feel that way. But you can. Here are some ways you can help fulfill the core needs in this chapter.

Finding good, hard-working candidates who want to grow within an organization is hard. When working on the Intentional Leadership Turn core need, it's not uncommon for employees of smaller businesses not to see how they will get promoted in the future. But as companies expand, so do the opportunities to find yourself in a new role; you just have to be ready for it. You can make yourself better suited for future roles by taking an interest in the company, sharing your opinions, and continuing to learn skills that will help you and the business.

To stay relevant, every company needs to be dynamic. The great companies adjust with quarterly dynamics. That can lead to a lot of change. Running a growing company means having to look at what's happening in the market and change accordingly. You can help with this by watching for changes and trends in the market and the world. Maybe you're hearing the same questions, doubts, and concerns from your customers—discuss what you're hearing with your manager.

Are you aware of any new technologies or ways to improve your operation? This is where the Ongoing Adaptation core need is fulfilled. Researching the tools and systems that will keep the company relevant is not the sole responsibility of the managers. They need help. On a cruise ship, all crew members have a duty to scan their environment for threats or potentially dangerous opportunities. Your goal is to watch for changes that could affect the company either positively or negatively.

In the Client Cooperation core need, we looked at the company that organized community service days to help its clients. What can your company do? Gather your coworkers and brainstorm ideas that will help your managers see potential ways for your company to be of service to your clients.

Now it's time to use your skills to improve your community or those you serve by fulfilling the Legacy of Contribution core need. By actively participating in the programs your leadership has set up, you will make a real difference, probably beyond what you thought was possible when you began reading this chapter.

Chapter 9

YOU'RE GONNA DO SOMETHING BIG

MY MATERNAL GRANDFATHER HOWARD AND I HAD A SPECIAL CONnection; I was like the son he never had. He was a delivery driver for Nabisco and drove a truck filled with the greatest cookies, which made him the coolest grandpa. But there was something else about him—he was my biggest supporter. He fed my entrepreneurial fire. He never owned a business, but he encouraged me, rooted for me, and inspired me to think bigger.

Grandpa Howard was a smoker, and Grandma Mary would not allow him to smoke in the house, so most of the time he smoked while sitting outside on the steps of his house. He had two sets of steps to choose from, one in the front and one on the side, and he alternated where he sat. When he was done smoking, he would flip his cigarette butt into the yard or a flowerbed. My grandmother tolerated this practice until she determined that the butts had become unsightly. At her breaking point she would yell, "Howard, pick up those damn butts." He would grumble about it and then go collect them for their final disposal.

At the age of six, I observed this cycle and realized that he had a problem: He needed an ashtray. But not just any ashtray, he needed a big one. On a mission to solve that problem, I went to my grandmother and asked her for the Planters peanut jar on the counter. At the time, the nuts were sold in glass containers about ten inches tall.

She handed me the peanut jar, which was about 25% full, and said, "Don't spoil your supper."

I informed her, "I just want the bottle, not the peanuts."

"What do you want the bottle for?"

"I want to make Granddaddy an ashtray."

Supportive of the idea, she emptied the remaining peanuts into another jar and handed me the empty one. I got to work. Next, I commandeered the aluminum foil. I shoved the foil into the opening, wrapping it around the top of the jar. The foil would hide the cigarette butts so that you could not see what was inside through the glass. The project was finished in no time, and I took it to my grandfather. "Here," I said, "I made you this ashtray. You can put your cigarettes in here instead of throwing them in the yard."

He said with a proud smile, "Well, thank you, son."

He placed the ashtray on the ground next to the steps to the side door where he sat having a smoke. When he was done, he used the new ashtray. I was proud as could be that I had solved a problem. I began telling my grandparents about how I was going to make more ashtrays. "Grandpa, you need one for the front doorstep."

He replied, "I sure do!"

Grandma knew that meant I would be on the hunt for another Planters jar. Before I knew it, I had secured another one and Grandpa had an ashtray at the front doorstep.

As my grandparents watched proudly, I declared, "I think I can sell these."

Smiling, Grandpa said, "You're gonna do something big!"

My ashtray production expanded; any neighbor I saw smoking became a prospect. They had a problem, and I planned to solve it—for a nominal fee, of course. Who could say no to the kid selling ashtrays door-to-door? I sold a few, but my supply chain was limited by how fast we could eat the peanuts. Also, my neighbors only needed one of my ashtrays, so my business fizzled out quickly.

I was always thinking about ways to make money, and Grandpa was a supporter. He would sit for hours listening to me talk about this or that idea. He would ground me in reality when he thought it necessary, but his true role was as my supporter, repeating, "You're gonna do something big!"

When I was ready to expand into mowing lawns, he offered his lawn mower and gas. I did the work and collected the money, and he purchased the gas for the mower; talk about high margins! When I struggled with a rough yard, he helped me finish, never wanting anything but to support me.

He taught me to play golf, paid for lessons, and fueled my dream of being a professional golfer. When I learned that to become a pro you need deep pockets or sponsors, he told me that if I got to that point, I would find the money and he would help me. "You're gonna do something big!"

My interest in business continued to grow. At fourteen, when I wanted to learn how to form a company, he drove me to the library to get a book on the topic. He drove me to the library a lot, and I read tons of business books. In college, when I was invited by my accounting professor to attend the Accounting Honor Society, Grandpa knew that I needed a suit, so we went to JCPenney and bought one. Driving home, he told me he was proud of me. "You're gonna do something big!"

Eventually, I met the girl who would become my wife, and when Grandpa passed, she assumed his role as my supporter, my cheerleader. Like Grandpa, she is unfailingly supportive of my ideas and my entrepreneurial desires. In 2014, when I told her I wanted to try real estate investing for the fifth time, she said, "Let's try it!" She knew that I wanted out of my corporate role and that my job was on the line.

I began this book with the story of my walk in Oklahoma City and how I wanted to replace my income before I was laid off. On February 10, 2016, I prepared for another conference call. I knew this one would be different, but I didn't know how different. Shortly before 10:00 a.m., I closed my office door and sat down at my desk. The CIO of the company joined the call. It sounded like he had prerecorded the message and they just played the recording. On the call, he announced that "almost all" of the IT functions of the company were being outsourced to IBM. I was taken aback. I did not see that coming. Through the glass next to my office door, I could see people covering their mouths in shock and some beginning to cry.

I hadn't realized that everyone in IT, all 500 of us, were on the call.

The CIO ended by saying, "Your manager will tell you if you are affected, and they will provide next steps."

My phone began to ring from one of my direct reports. He asked, "Are we affected?"

"I don't know, I will get back to you," I reassured him.

I opened my door and walked out. The new leaders, you know, the friends of the CIO, well, they were all conveniently out of the office that day. Walking out of my office and into the common area, I felt numb. It felt like a bomb had gone off and I was walking through the carnage. Groups of people were gathering, many sobbing. I spotted more people from my team and walked toward them. Not knowing what to say, I told them, "I know this is hard, but it will be OK, we will all be OK."

One of them asked sharply, "Did you know?"

"No, I found out just like you. I don't know what this means and if we are affected, but I will let you know."

I walked back to my office, my heart racing. *What am I going to do?*

Suddenly, I was filled with a sense of peace. While my real estate business was not 100% ready to support my family, it was close. *I will be OK*, I thought.

I called my boss, and he confirmed that me and my team were affected by the outsourcing and that I would be needed for six weeks to help with the transition. In exchange, I would be given six months of severance. He ended the call by saying, "You'll have a great career, just not here."

I have seven months and two weeks of paychecks remaining, I thought. *I need to move my business further along.* If I treated it like my full-time job, I knew I could get it to support us.

During the next six weeks, I spent all my time working on it. My corporate office became my real estate investing headquarters. When I was needed for my job, I was available, but the rest of the time I focused on my business, which continued to grow. By my last day on the job, the recurring positive cash flows from the business exceeded my salary. I had replaced my income. I was excited and scared!

At 11:58 a.m., I grabbed my briefcase, walked to the door of my office and gave it one last look. I turned off the lights, shut the door, and took what felt like the first step toward achieving my goal.

My walk to the car was filled with a mix of emotions. On the one hand, I was excited. I had made it! A mere seventeen months and three days after I started my real estate investing business, I was free from corporate America. On the other hand, there were no guarantees. As Jonathan said in the introduction, "I and I alone would determine how my business would succeed or fail."

I had a short drive to the lunch spot where I was meeting my wife. I parked the car, exited the vehicle, and walked to where she stood waiting outside the restaurant. She smiled as I approached her, but each step I took toward her made it harder for me to smile. I was scared.

As I got closer, she extended her arms for a hug, and as I leaned into her, she wrapped her arms around me and I was rewarded with the biggest, tightest hug—I call it my victory hug. She declared, "You did it, you achieved your dream, you work for yourself now! I'm so proud of you! Your grandfather would be so proud of you."

Grandpa's words rushed back to me. *You're gonna do something big!*

Tears began to form. I had achieved victory. I had conquered the mountain. I was victorious in my pursuit. I had defied the odds.

This story is not about my Grandpa Howard, or me. This story is about you. I want this moment for you; this is what you're working toward. You are now equipped with a framework to guide you and your business to the highest levels of your aspiration.

You, dear reader, you're gonna do something big!

Starting with the IPP assessment, you will determine what your business needs most right now. You and your team will not try to handle everything, and you will stop putting out fires. Instead, you will identify which problem you need to fix next and begin to address that vital need. You will solve it. Then you will take the IPP assessment again and move on to the next vital need.

You will not try to scale the IPP because you know it's impossible. Today you could be working on Impact-level needs; tomorrow you might have to drop back down to Deal Flow. Give the business what it needs.

You will use the IPP to avoid the survival trap, so you don't make decisions just to survive. With the IPP as your trusted source of direction, you will address the problems your business is facing now. You will solve the most important vital need, fixing the weakest link in your process, your team, and your business, and then you will move on to the next one. Your business will continue to grow.

You will take the IPP assessment again and again, to the point where it becomes second nature. You will take the assessment so many times that you won't need to look at the questions in this book; they will be in your mind. The questions will create a flow and you will be able to run through the IPP quickly, knowing what to address next. The IPP and the core needs will serve as the common language of your business. Why? Because you're gonna do something big!

From Deal Flow to Profit to Order and back to Profit, you will move from vital need to vital need. You need this business to work and so does the world. Your employees need you to build a business that supports your lifestyle. They know that when your needs are met, you will be able to present them with life-changing opportunities. You're gonna do something big!

On rough days, when you're facing the inner critic-trolls, the IPP and its simple framework will be your guiding light. You will know what to work on and what to ignore. You will remind yourself that all businesses have problems, and not all problems are important.

And when you achieve your financial and time freedom goals, you will move onward to Impact, where you become a transformational force for your team, your customers, and your community. You will then have the resources, the team, and the freedom to leave a legacy for future generations because you are the steward of the business.

As for me, I'm right here rooting for you, shouting, "You're gonna do something big!" How big?

Bigger than you can imagine in this moment.

Bigger than your wildest, most impossible dreams.

Bigger than the doubts that currently hold you back.

Bigger than the limits you place on yourself.

Because when you live your purpose, what you achieve isn't big— it's limitless.

ENDNOTES

INTRODUCTION

[1] Einar H. Dyvik, "Established business ownership rate in North America in 2023, by country," Statista, July 04, 2024, https://www.statista.com/statistics/315556/established-business-ownership-rate-in-north-america/, last accessed May 11, 2025.

CHAPTER 1

[2] @gregoryknox4444, "JFK Jr.'s Final Flight | Mayday Air Disaster," YouTube, https://www.youtube.com/watch?v=6_fJuzWH-h8, last accessed October 18, 2024.

[3] Melchor J. Antunano, "Spatial Disorientation: Why You Shouldn't Fly By the Seat of Your Pants," Federal Aviation Administration, https://www.faa.gov/pilots/safety/pilotsafetybrochures/media/spatiald.pdf, last accessed May 11, 2025.

[4] Cell Press, "With Nothing To Guide Their Way, People Really Do Walk In Circles," ScienceDaily, August 21, 2009, https://www.sciencedaily.com/releases/2009/08/090820123927.htm, last accessed May 11, 2025.

[5] Mike Michalowicz, *Fix This Next: Make the Vital Change That Will Level Up Your Business* (New York, NY: Portfolio, 2020).

[6] Michalowicz, *Fix This Next*

CHAPTER 2

[7] Eliyahu M. Goldratt, *The Goal: A Process of Ongoing Improvement* (Great Barrington, MA: The North River Press Publishing Corporation, 2014).

[8] *Seinfeld*, season 5, episode 22, "The Opposite," aired May 19, 1994, on NBC, directed by Tom Cherones, written by Larry David, Jerry Seinfeld, and Andy Cowan.

[9] "Building a Unicorn: How to Launch, Fund, and Scale a Startup," Wharton Online, https://online-execed.wharton.upenn.edu/building-unicorn, last accessed May 11, 2025.

[10] U.S. Department of Housing and Urban Development, Office of Policy Development and Research, "Spotlight on the Housing Market in the Detroit-Warren-Livonia, Michigan MSA," January 2013, https://archives.huduser.gov/scorecard/pdf/Spotlight-Detroit-Warren-Livonia.pdf, last accessed May 11, 2025.

[11] Peter F. Drucker, *The Practice of Management* (New York, NY: HarperCollins, 1986).

[12] Brian Schuldt, "27 companies that use OKRs and success stories," Tability, https://www.tability.io/odt/articles/companies-that-use-okrs-and-success-stories, last accessed May 11, 2025.

CHAPTER 3

[13] "Zillow Research Data," Zillow, https://www.zillow.com/research/data/, last accessed September 22, 2024.

[14] Michalowicz, *Fix This Next*

[15] *Wayne's World*, directed by Penelope Spheeris (Paramount Pictures, 1992).

[16] Paco Underhill, *Why We Buy: The Science of Shopping* (New York, NY: Simon & Schuster, 1999).

CHAPTER 4

[17] Michalowicz, *Fix This Next*

[18] Mike Michalowicz, *Profit First: Transform Your Business from a Cash-Eating Monster to a Money-Making Machine* (New York, NY: Portfolio [reissue edition], 2017.

[19] David Richter, *Profit First for Real Estate Investing: Transform Your Business from a Cash-Eating Monster to a Money-Making Machine* (St. Cloud, FL: Simple CFO Solutions, LLC, 2021).

[20] Warren Cassell Jr., "Who Is Dave Ramsey?" Investopedia, updated August 20, 2015, https://www.investopedia.com/articles/investing/082015/how-dave-ramsey-made-his-fortune.asp, last accessed May 11, 2025.

[21] Michalowicz, *Fix This Next*

[22] Mortgage Bankers Association, "Total Commercial Real Estate Borrowing and Lending Declined 47 Percent in 2023," April 23, 2024, https://www.mba.org/news-and-research/newsroom/news/2024/04/23/total-commercial-and-multifamily-borrowing-and-lending-expected-to-fall-to-684-billion-in-2023, last accessed May 11, 2025.

[23] Michalowicz, *Fix This Next*

[24] Michalowicz, *Fix This Next*

[25] Alun Rhydderch, "Scenario Building: The 2x2 Matrix Technique," ResearchGate, June 2017, https://www.researchgate.net/publication/331564544_Scenario_Building_The_2x2_Matrix_Technique, last accessed May 11, 2025.

CHAPTER 5

[26] Randall Lane, "Bezos Unbound: Exclusive Interview with the Amazon Founder on What He Plans to Conquer Next," *Forbes*, August 30, 2018 (cover story of the September 2018 print issue).

[27] Jina Kim and Hye-Sun Jung, "The Effect of Employee Competency and Organizational Culture on Employees' Perceived Stress for Better Workplace," *PubMed Central*, April 7, 2022, https://pmc.ncbi.nlm.nih.gov/articles/PMC9032235/, last accessed May 11, 2025.

[28] Brian Sutter, "How Hard Small Business Owners Work," SCORE, April 13, 2019, https://www.score.org/resource/blog-post/how-hard-small-business-owners-work, last accessed May 11, 2025.

[29] Mike Michalowicz, *Clockwork: Design Your Business to Run Itself* (New York, NY: Portfolio, 2018).

CHAPTER 6

[30] Blake Mycoskie, "How I Did It: The TOMS Story," Entrepreneur, https://www.entrepreneur.com/business-news/who-is-blake-mycoskie-how-he-created-toms-shoes-brand/220350, last accessed May 11, 2025.

[31] David Hessekiel, "The Rise and Fall of the Buy-One-Give-One Model at TOMS," Forbes, April 28, 2021, https://www.forbes.com/sites/davidhessekiel/2021/04/28/the-rise-and-fall-of-the-buy-one-give-one-model-at-toms/, last accessed May 11, 2025.

[32] "TOMS Impact Report," TOMS, https://www.toms.com/en-gb/impact/report, last accessed December 13, 2024.

[33] Giovanni Rossi, Mark Dingemanse, Simeon Floyd, Julija Baranova, Joe Blythe, Kobin H. Kendrick, Jörg Zinken, and N. J. Enfield, "Shared crosscultural principles underlie human prosocial behavior at the smallest scale," *Scientific Reports* 13, no. 6057 (2023), https://doi.org/10.1038/s41598-023-30580-5, last accessed May 11, 2025.

CHAPTER 7

[34] Matthew Kelly, *The Dream Manager* (New York, NY: Hyperion, 2007).

[35] Caroline Garrow, "The Truth Behind Talent Retention and the Importance of Healthy Management," Talent Evolution Group, October 30, 2023, https://www.talentevolutiongroup.com/talent-insights/blog/truth-behind-talent-retention/, last accessed September 30, 2024.

[36] Adwords Nerds, "Episode #107 – Mastering Networking for Real Estate with Andrew Dunn," Adwords Nerds, September 09, 2020, https://adwordsnerds.com/episode-107-mastering-networking-for-real-estate-with-andrew-dunn/, last accessed May 11, 2025.

[37] "The Road to Abundance—Innovation, Disruption, and Opportunity: 2016 IRI Medal Address." *Research-Technology Management* 59, no. 6 (November 2016): 12-18.

[38] Michalowicz, *Fix This Next*

CHAPTER 8

[39] Cornell SC Johnson College of Business, "Family Business Facts," Cornell SC Johnson College of Business, https://business.cornell.edu/centers/smith/resources/family-business-facts/, last accessed May 11, 2025.

[40] DeBartolo Family Foundation, "About Our Foundation," DeBartolo Family Foundation, updated 2024, https://debartolofamilyfoundation.org/about/, last accessed May 11, 2025.

[41] Karen Smith, "Phildra Swagger Turned Her Dream Into a Reality with Brooks-DeBartolo," Patch, June 28, 2011, https://patch.com/florida/templeterrace/phildra-swagger-turned-her-dream-into-a-reality-with-ab7eb498a2, last accessed May 11, 2025.

ACKNOWLEDGMENTS

[42] Kathleen Elkins, "Warren Buffett says the most important decision you'll ever make has nothing to do with your money or career," CNBC.com, May 14, 2018, https://www.cnbc.com/2018/05/14/warren-buffett-says-the-most-important-decision-is-who-you-marry.html, last accessed May 11, 2025.

ACKNOWLEDGMENTS

WRITING A BOOK IS A WEIRD EXPERIENCE; YOU SIT AT THE KEY-board for hours typing your thoughts, knowledge, and stories, hoping that readers will love it, never knowing for sure but believing that for the right audience, your message will be exactly what they need on their journey.

In the process, you also realize just how many people have helped bring your thoughts to life. I can't possibly list all the people I need to thank for their friendship, leadership, and time throughout the years. However, there are some key people that I need to thank because if it weren't for them, this book would still be in my head.

Our lives are influenced by many people who contribute to our experience from behind the scenes; they facilitate our success, seek no glory, and only want to help others. AJ Harper, Laura Stone, and Sadé Amherd at Top Three Book Workshop are great examples. They get no spotlight, yet the books they help bring to life are in the hundreds. The three of you help transform dreamers into authors, and our readers benefit from your mission. Thank you for showing me how to be an author.

I can't think of a single business author who has impacted entrepreneurs as much as Mike Michalowicz. No one can deny your contribution to the entrepreneur and business communities, Mike. Your books have transformed so many lives and saved so many businesses. Thank you for writing *Fix This Next*, and for allowing me to extend its message to my investing friends.

Mike practices what he preaches and has built a fantastic team so he is not his business's linchpin. Amy Cartelli is one of those great people and was instrumental in supporting this book. From getting messages to Mike to making decisions while he was on yet another four-week vacation (I told you he's legit) to overseeing the book cover and the various permissions and contract, this book may not have been written if it weren't for her. Thank you, Amy.

Thank you to my editor, Zoë Bird. You delivered on your promise to enhance my message, voice, and style, and I thank you for your contribution to this book.

In 2014, I needed to replace my income, and Mark Podolsky, aka The Land Geek, appeared in my life to guide me on my journey. We quickly built a bond, and since that time, our friendship has turned into a fantastic business partnership. Mark, you have stated that your mission is to eliminate solo economic dependency. I can't think of a better person to take on that challenge. Your commitment to that mission is inspiring, and I appreciate your friendship and brotherhood. Keep changing lives, brother.

It's incredible to watch future business leaders evolve, and Tate Litchfield, it has been remarkable to watch you transform from a young investor into the rock star leader you are today. You are such a vital part of the team, and I'm thankful every day that I get to work with you and call you my friend.

I was blessed with an incredible mom, Linda. You have been the best mom to me—always supportive, ready to talk, and excited to hear about my life. Thank you, Mom, for everything, including ensuring that I get at least one five-star review.

I have some important family members in heaven who are vital to how I see the world: my father Benjamin, grandfather Howard, and grandmother Mary. I'm grateful for the time I spent with each of you; it was not long enough.

To my children, Hope and Cole: You can't imagine how proud I am of both of you. Watching you grow into the strong adults you have become is one of the greatest gifts of my life. I can't wait to see what you do next.

According to psychologists from Carnegie Mellon University, "People with supportive spouses are "more likely to give themselves the chance to succeed."[42] Thankfully, my wife Kristine fulfills that role. In the last chapter, I mentioned how she replaced Grandpa as my biggest cheerleader, and I'm indeed a better man because of her. Writing some of these chapters was a challenge, and one day at lunch, I was telling her how difficult it was. True to her supportive nature, she grabbed my forearm tightly and declared, "You've got this." Kristine, I'm grateful every day for you and our family. Thank you for being my rock, for supporting me, and for my second five-star review.

ABOUT THE AUTHOR

B. SCOTT TODD IS A REAL ESTATE INVESTOR AND SEASONED ENTRE-
preneur with a passion for helping others grow their businesses. With
a background as a former vice president at a Fortune 500 company,
Scott brings a rare blend of corporate leadership, street-smart investing, and operational excellence to everything he does.

After starting and scaling multiple businesses—including a leading
land-purchasing platform—Scott turned his focus to solving one of
the biggest challenges facing real estate investors: knowing what to
fix next. Through thousands of conversations with investors, he has
seen firsthand how investors can get stuck fixing the wrong problems, wasting time, money and momentum. And he believes that
every investor has the power to build a business that funds their life
instead of consuming it. That's why he wrote *Fix This Next for Real
Estate Investors*.

Connect with Scott at:

🌐 www.ScottTodd.net